GREAT BOOK *of*
CELTIC
Patterns

Second Edition,
Revised and Expanded

THE ULTIMATE DESIGN SOURCEBOOK
FOR ARTISTS AND CRAFTERS

GREAT BOOK *of* CELTIC Patterns

Second Edition, *Revised and Expanded*

THE ULTIMATE DESIGN SOURCEBOOK FOR ARTISTS AND CRAFTERS

by Lora S. Irish

FOX CHAPEL
PUBLISHING

Acknowledgments

Special thanks go to Alan Giagnocavo, Peg Couch, Gretchen Bacon,
Troy Thorne, Lindsay Hess, Chanyn DeShong, and everyone at Fox Chapel Publishing
who worked on this project. Their encouragement and support throughout the
creation of this book have been indispensable. It has, once again, been a delight
for me to work with such a well-organized and creative team. And thanks to Laura Taylor
and David Fisk at Fox Chapel for their work on this Second Edition.

—Lora S. Irish

© 2007, 2018 by Lora S. Irish and Fox Chapel Publishing Company, Inc., 903 Square Street, Mount Joy, PA 17552.

Great Book of Celtic Patterns, Second Edition, Revised and Expanded (2018) is a revised edition of *Great Book of Celtic Patterns* (2007), published by Fox Chapel Publishing Company, Inc. Revisions include new photographs and new patterns. The patterns contained herein are copyrighted by the author. Readers may make copies of these patterns for personal use. The patterns themselves, however, are not to be duplicated for resale or distribution under any circumstances. Any such copying is a violation of copyright law.

ISBN 978-1-56523-926-5

Library of Congress Cataloging-in-Publication Data

Names: Irish, Lora S., author.
Title: Great book of Celtic patterns / Lora S. Irish.
Description: Second edition, revised and expanded. | Mount Joy : Fox Chapel
  Publishing, 2018. | Includes index.
Identifiers: LCCN 2017033486 | ISBN 9781565239265 (pbk.)
Subjects: LCSH: Knotwork, Celtic. | Handicraft--Patterns.
Classification: LCC NK1264 .I75 2018 | DDC 746.42/2041089916--dc23
LC record available at https://lccn.loc.gov/2017033486

To learn more about the other great books from Fox Chapel Publishing, or to find a retailer near you, call toll-free
800-457-9112 or visit us at *www.FoxChapelPublishing.com*.

We are always looking for talented authors. To submit an idea, please send a brief inquiry to
acquisitions@foxchapelpublishing.com.

Printed in China
First printing

Lora S. Irish is a nationally known artist and author, whose books include *Landscapes in Relief*, *Wildlife Carving in Relief*, *North American Wildlife Patterns for the Scroll Saw*, *World Wildlife Patterns for the Scroll Saw*, *Great Book of Dragon Patterns*, *Great Book of Fairy Patterns*, *Great Book of Floral Patterns*, *Wood Spirits and Green Men*, and *Great Book of Woodburning*. She is also a frequent contributor to *Woodcarving Illustrated* and *Scroll Saw Woodworking & Crafts*. Twelve of the author's purebred dog breed oil canvas paintings have been published as limited editions.

Working from their home studio, Lora and her husband and webmaster, Michael, are the owners of three websites: *LSIrish.com, ArtDesignsStudio.com*, and *www.carvingpatterns.com*. Classic Carving Patterns is their Internet woodcarving studio, focusing on online tutorials, projects, and patterns created exclusively by the author for the crafter and artisan.

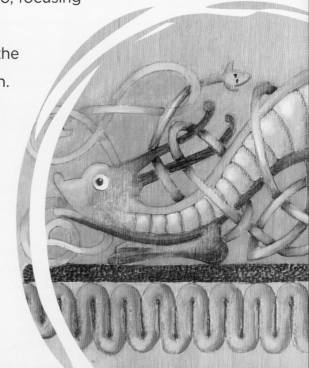

Contents

FROM THE AUTHOR/ARTIST..VIII

HOW TO USE THIS BOOK...IX

CHAPTER 1   THE ORIGINS OF CELTIC KNOTS......................1
An introduction to the history of interlocking and interlacing line designs

CHAPTER 2   GALLERY..9
Using Celtic knot work in various media

CHAPTER 3   CELTIC LINE AND KNOT PATTERNS.................33
Understanding twists, braids, and knotted lines

CHAPTER 4   PLOTTING AND GRAPHING KNOTS.................41
Using graph paper to create and modify knotted lines

CHAPTER 5   LAYOUT IDEAS..55
Creating borders, corners, and multiple interlocking knots

CHAPTER 6   PATTERN CHANGES...................................61
Altering designs to work within a specific layout or space

CHAPTER 7   FINIALS FOR INTERLOCKING DESIGNS..........65
Using animals, leaves, and scrolls to finish knotted lines

CHAPTER 8   LINE ENHANCEMENTS...............................77
Adding accents and interior designs to create more complex, textured patterns

CHAPTER 9   ADDING COLOR.......................................83
A step-by-step guide to enhancing your work with color

CHAPTER 10 CELTIC KNOT PATTERNS......................................91
Line Patterns 92
Corner Patterns 108
Circles, Squares, and Motifs 121
Viking Animals 144
Finials 170
Variations on Line Texture 176
Fantasy 182
Religious Symbols 206

GLOSSARY OF TERMS...215

INDEX...218

From the Author/Artist

Growing up in a family full of craftsmen and artisans, I had no doubt that I would focus my attention on the arts. It seemed that there was always something being created in my childhood home. The dining room table was often full of newly cut quilt pieces, ceramic bisque and glazes, or plans for the most recent woodworking furniture endeavor. I can remember the pieces of an old muzzle-loading rifle submerged in a butter tub of oil, waiting for restoration, while the barrel, coated with bluing, hung from the patio door curtain rod and the gun stock sat ready to be carved.

Not hidden in some basement or workshop, all the creating seemed to happen right in the living room or dining room. Wonderful smells are associated with these memories: turpentine and linseed oil, cedar wood and walnut for carving, newly bought calico fabrics, and the makings for strawberry jelly on the stove.

My house, just like my mom's, is filled with art and craft supplies. A basket of cloth and thread sits on the floor next to my living room chair. The yarn ball basket rests across the room in the corner with the needles and hooks ready for the next afghan to be started. My studio area is stuffed with boxes and totes full of paints, canvases and papers, glue, scissors, and accessories.

When Fox Chapel offered me the opportunity to do a book that focused on presenting techniques and patterns for Celtic knot work, it seemed to be the perfect new project. In my experience, few artisans do just one craft or one style of art. Many of us enjoy a wide variety of creative endeavors. And many of us already have a strong understanding of our favorite art; all we really need are new ideas and patterns with which to express ourselves.

How to use this book

As you work through the pages of this book, you will see that there are no spiral, key pattern, or geometric designs included here. These excellent design motifs belong to the pre-Christian Celtic era. However, because the pre-Christian era covers such a broad span of time and development, I decided to narrow the focus of this book to Celtic art from 700 AD to 1150 AD. During this time, the Vikings invaded the British Isles and influenced Celtic art. The modern Celtic art so popular today can be traced back to the interlaced knot patterns that appear on the early illuminated manuscripts, a direct result of the influence of the Viking culture on the British Isles.

We will start by exploring the basics of the knotted line, including simple twists and braids, plus one-line and multiple-line knot patterns. Knotted line patterns can include inserted units, such as squares, circles, and hearts, and they can be created by interlocking self-contained knot patterns.

Once you have an understanding of the way knot patterns can be created, we will go step-by-step through the process of plotting and graphing a basic knot design. This will teach you how to adapt the patterns in this book to your craft or project and how to graph your own new knot designs. Once the knot pattern is created, we will explore how that knot can be incorporated into different styles of pattern layouts, including squares, circles, line work, and corner ideas.

Celtic knot work often contains split lines, tendrils, and finials, and we will study techniques to create these elements next. The lines within a Celtic knot can change in the middle of the pattern. They can change size, becoming thinner or thicker than in other areas of the work. They can also suddenly split into two or more thin lines with those lines then reattaching or reuniting in one line. Because not all Celtic knots are closed or self-contained, you will learn how to add ornamentation or animal motif heads to the open ends of your knot work.

Knot work and interlocked or interlaced line designs are not constrained just to Celtic art; they appear in almost every art style and throughout art history. Early Greek bas-relief carvings show long, thin plant stems that flow from one area of the work to another, crossing over other stems in a twist pattern. The Romanesque period of ornamentation heavily incorporates the interlocking line design, often with heavy foliage and turned-back leaves. Early Russian designs show the knotted design as both stylized line patterns and as intricate repeating motifs. Even the Victorian era used the interlaced line to create entwined vines of floral sprays, and, during the late German Renaissance, this motif appears as highly detailed ironwork. So, as we explore the idea of adding finials to your Celtic knot designs, we will also look at how different historical art styles can use the Celtic knot work as the basis for their design.

Finally, we will work through the variations that the line itself can incorporate, including texturing, pattern work, and even rope designs. So let's begin our journey through the knotted path of Celtic art by first exploring the origins of the art.

CHAPTER 1

The Origins of Celtic Knots

AN INTRODUCTION TO THE HISTORY OF INTERLOCKING AND INTERLACING LINE DESIGNS

Today's Celtic knot work, the topic of this book, features complex designs that developed over several centuries in Scotland, Ireland, Wales, and North England, with strong influences from the Viking culture. The first examples of knot work in Celtic art appeared after the first Viking invasions of Britain circa 800 AD. The Viking influence upon Celtic art continued through six stages of Viking artwork until 1150 AD. In this chapter, we'll take a look at illuminated manuscripts—writings that were embellished with hand-decorated and gold-leafed borders, letters, and illustrations—of the Christian Bible and explore the merging of these different cultural art styles into what is known today as Celtic knot work.

Early Celtic art

Figure 1.1. The earliest Celtic designs were created using the most basic of geometric shapes and patterns.

Early Celtic art, or pre-Christian Celtic art, consisted of spiral, maze, and key pattern designs (see **Figure 1.1**). Key patterns are often described as either angular maze designs or straight-line spirals. Zigzag patterns and diamond designs were common during this period. These geometric shapes did not include the interlocking line designs or the animal motifs that are associated with Celtic knot work today.

In 635 AD, an Irish monk named Aidan was summoned by King Oswald of Northumbria to be the bishop of the northern area of King Oswald's lands. Aidan, a Scots-Celtic monk from the Isle of Iona, established his monastery on an isolated island named Lindisfarne. His life was devoted to converting the Northumbrians to Christianity.

By the time of St. Aidan's arrival at Lindisfarne, the earliest illuminated manuscripts were already being created. Around 575 AD, a copy of the Psalms called the *Cathach of St. Colmcille* (Columba) was written. St. Colmcille, the author and scribe associated with this early work, decorated the manuscript with enlarged, ornate, initial lettering. The initial letters in the manuscript use the pre-Christian Celtic art style of spirals, zigzag lines, and curved line shapes but no interlocking knots or line designs.

Viking influences on Celtic art

In 700 AD, the Vikings, warriors from the north, began their movement into Europe, then into England and Ireland. It was in 793 AD that Lindisfarne experienced the first Viking raid on Britain. These raids continued until 875 AD when the monks fled the island.

The *Book of Kells*, scribed by Irish monks, is probably the most noted of the illuminated Christian manuscripts and includes the four Gospels written in Latin. Work on this book began around 800 AD. The book is often associated with Iona and Northumbria, where the writing was begun, but it is now closely associated with the Kells monastery, located thirty miles northwest of Dublin, Ireland. All but two of the manuscript's 680 pages are richly decorated with pre-Christian Celtic spiral and key pattern art, interlaced Viking animals, and Celtic knot patterns (see **Figure 1.2** and **Figure 1.3**). Animals and knot patterns are twisted or incorporated to become initial letters of sections of the text. So the *Book of Kells* shows the blending of the pre-Christian Celtic art with the Viking influence that had established itself in the British Isles by the time of its writing.

Figure 1.2. This page from the *Book of Kells* features the symbols for the four evangelists. Matthew is represented by the man, Mark by the lion, Luke by the calf, and John by the eagle.

Figure 1.3. This page, often called the Chi Rho page, begins Matthew's description of the nativity. In addition to the knot work present in the letters, the page also contains a number of animals and people.

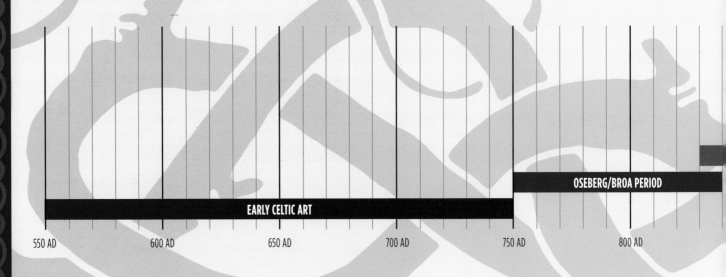

OSEBERG/BROA PERIOD

EARLY CELTIC ART

550 AD   600 AD   650 AD   700 AD   750 AD   800 AD

550 AD – 750 AD
Early Celtic Art

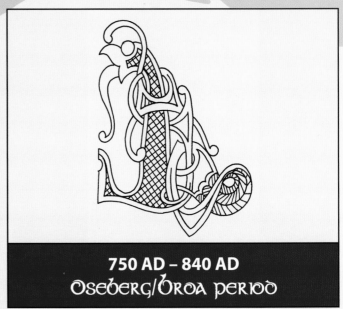

750 AD – 840 AD
Oseberg/Broa Period

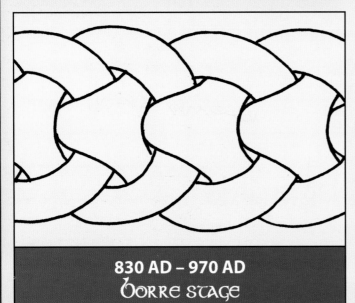

830 AD – 970 AD
Borre Stage

880 AD – 1000 AD
Jelling Stage

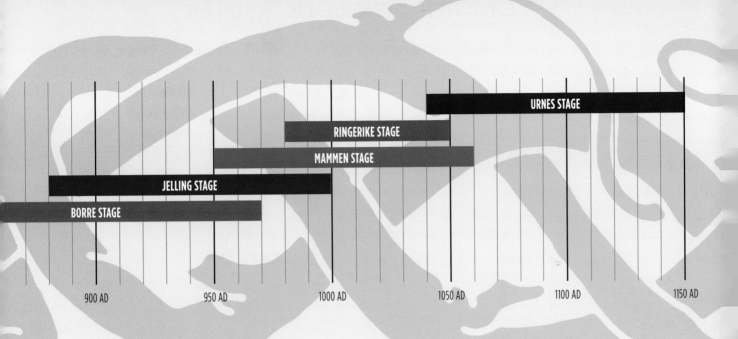

BORRE STAGE

JELLING STAGE

MAMMEN STAGE

RINGERIKE STAGE

URNES STAGE

900 AD   950 AD   1000 AD   1050 AD   1100 AD   1150 AD

950 AD – 1060 AD
Mammen Stage

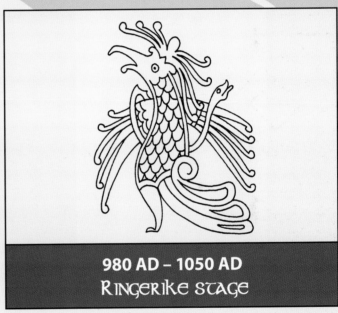

980 AD – 1050 AD
Ringerike Stage

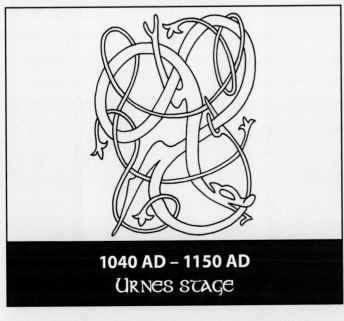

1040 AD – 1150 AD
Urnes Stage

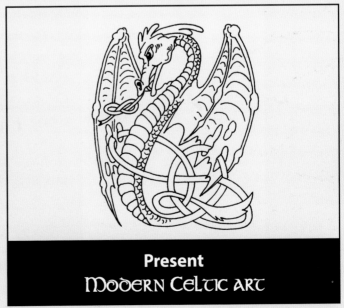

Present
Modern Celtic Art

Figure 1.4. Early Viking animals had little resemblance to the animals they represented.

The **Oseberg/Broa period**, between 750 AD and 840 AD, is considered the first of the Viking art stages. Animals have small heads and extra-wide bodies created with curved lines. Often, an animal cannot be identified as one particular species (see **Figure 1.4**). Geometric patterns are used to surround the animal motifs. The most notable Viking animal of this stage is called the Gripping Beast or Great Beast, often taking on a dragonlike appearance.

Between 830 AD and 970 AD, Viking art moved into its second stage: the **Borre stage**. Animal bodies become thinner, more ribbonlike, and begin to intertwine or twist within the design. Curved bodies begin to arch sharply. During this stage the ring-chain pattern is notable and is one of the first interlocking repetitive designs of Celtic knot work. This is the first appearance of the interlocking knot design as part of an animal's body or as a stand-alone pattern (see **Figure 1.5**).

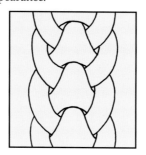

Figure 1.5. Interlocking patterns, such as this chain mail sample, began to appear during the Borre Stage.

The **Jelling stage**, the third stage of Viking art, probably had the greatest influence on the Celtic art of today. Between 880 AD and 1000 AD, the Viking animal designs become intricate in both their interlacing and their decorations (see **Figure 1.6**). The

Figure 1.6. By 1000 AD, the animal form had matured into distinct and intricate patterns.

ribbon bodies of the animal during this period begin to contain their own decoration of simple circles, stripes, or geometric patterns. The mouths of the animals are opened and their lips are extended to become small knot patterns. Spiral designs accent hip joints and jaw lines.

The fourth stage of Viking art is called the **Mammen stage**, circa 950 AD to 1060 AD. More realistic or natural animals replace the stylized animals of earlier work. Yet the bodies of these animals now include very complex decorations of lines, dots, and stripes (see **Figure 1.7**). The spiral patterns along the hip joint and jaw line become more exaggerated. Plants and leaves begin to appear in the artwork. The feet of an animal may often be hard to distinguish because they can take on the appearance of two or three plant leaves.

Figure 1.7. Viking animals can create interlocking shapes with their bodies, and those bodies can contain patterns and designs.

By 980 AD and through 1050 AD, both animals and knot work appear. This is the **Ringerike stage**, the fifth stage of Viking art. Small, thin tendrils are added to the designs. These thinner lines split from either the line work or the animal's body to curve and curl independently (see **Figure 1.8**). The animal bodies lose much of their interior decoration, and the eyes begin to take on a strong almond shape. More elaborate foliage appears, as does the use of plants and vines as framework to the main design.

Between 1040 AD and 1150 AD, animals can

Figure 1.8. The Ringerike stage shows the heavily decorated body designs of the animals.

include more than one head, and snake heads, serpents, and dragon heads are often part of the pattern. The open mouths established during the Jelling stage now grip or bite other animals, or the

Figure 1.9. Late Viking animals contain both thick and thin line work, which often creates a random knotting pattern. Heads often turn back to grasp the legs or tail.

head and neck of the animal turn back upon itself to grasp its own legs or tail (see **Figure 1.9**). The round eyes of the earlier stages have been replaced with almond eyes. The spiral hip joints become minimal yet still remain. By this stage, animals have become the Celtic knot pattern, their bodies interlaced upon themselves and with other animals or inserted geometric designs. This sixth or last period of Viking art is called the **Urnes stage**.

A NOTE ABOUT SYMBOLISM

Viking animals are an important part of the Celtic knot work design style. The major animals include deer, wolves, birds, and dragonlike creatures. Snakes are often found in Viking knot work, but many of the early animals are so stylized that they cannot be identified. Both the Celtic culture and the Viking culture believed that adorning an object with an animal gave that object the strength or attributes of the animal shown, yet there is no evidence that individual animal motifs had special symbolism, spiritual powers, or association with specific gods, deities, or mythological stories. Nor do any individual knot patterns hold a symbolic meaning. Animals, animal knot work, and line knot work can be used interchangeably to create a Celtic design, and all three can appear within one pattern.

Modern Celtic art

One of the last major Viking raids occurred in 1066 when the Saxon King Harold Godwinson, an Anglicized Viking, defeated the Viking army led by Harald Hardrade. Ironically, Godwinson was defeated later in the same year by William, the Duke of Normandy, and his invading army. William was also of Viking descent.

Although the earliest Vikings arrived in the British Isles as invaders, Scandinavian peoples, including the Vikings, later settled into the area as farmers, establishing villages and small towns. Dublin, Ireland, was originally a Viking settlement. Before the Viking people were absorbed into the British culture, around the eleventh century, they would expand their area of influence into the Byzantine Empire, establish trade with Arab merchants, and create trade routes into the Middle East.

Figure 1.10. Today's Celtic and Viking animals can incorporate some or all of the elements of the interlocking Celtic knot.

Considering the pre-Christian Celtic love for repetitive geometric patterns, spiral turns, and flowing curved lines, it is easy to understand how the Celtic artists of Ireland, Scotland, Wales, and North Britain would embrace the intricate knot designs and animal motifs of the Vikings. Today's Celtic knot is an incorporation of all the cultures that inhabited the British Isles during the eighth through twelfth centuries (see **Figure 1.10**).

CHAPTER 2

Gallery

Now that you understand the history of Celtic knot work, let's take a look at some examples of knots used in different media to get you thinking about how you might want to use Celtic art in your particular craft. You will find a variety of knot work on these pages, everything from simple twists and braids to complex interlacings and large knotted designs. As you browse through the examples, you'll notice that Celtic knot work can stand alone or be part of an overall piece of art and that the interlocking and interlacing designs can also form a framework for other art. I've also pointed out how elements from the six stages of Viking history have influenced some of the designs.

Dragon Flight, a modern-style Celtic design, uses three separate knotting patterns to create the final design. The background border is a composite of several knots to make the rectangular frame for the dragon. The wing tips of the dragon in the mid-ground are interlaced in a simple trellis pattern. The dragon's tail then knots in the foreground to capture the background border design. This project was worked in artist oil paints on canvas and measures 12″ x 24″ (30 x 61 cm). The pattern for this project can be found on page 194.

In *Green Man, Wolves, and Birds Panel*, the Green Man face is surrounded by a complex braided knot pattern that transforms into Viking wolves. To add interest below the face, two Ringerike-style roosters with entwined tails grip the knot border. To complement the frame size of the *Dragon Flight* painting, the *Green Man, Wolves, and Birds Panel* was painted in artist oils on a 12" x 18" (30 x 46 cm) canvas. That canvas was matted with chocolate brown, and a small wolf line accent worked in colored pencil finished off the overset area. The pattern for this project can be found on page 188.

This *Backgammon Board* pattern was perfect for woodburning. The burn was worked on ¼″ x 12″ x 24″ (.64 x 30 x 61 cm) birch plywood. When the design was completed, the large areas inside the board were painted using artist acrylics. Then, the board was finished with two coats of Danish oil. The framing around this board makes it into a beautiful piece of wall art when the board is not being used. The pattern for this project can be found on page 204.

The *Horse and Dragon Chessboard* complements *Backgammon Board*. This one was also worked by first woodburning the design into birch plywood. Watercolors were used to create the shaded coloring of the board without losing any of the woodburned tones. Danish oil was applied, and the board was framed. The chessboard, too, will become wall art when not in use. The Urnes-style dragon header shows the use of thick and thin lines during that time period. The pattern for this project can be found on page 182.

Many a Welsh sailor spent his time at sea carving love spoons for those he left behind. The *Four-Line Twined Heart Spoon* (left) shows a simple entrapped heart within a lattice knot design. The *Lattice Spatula* (right) uses the heart pattern at the top of the spoon. Both spoons were carved from ¾" (2 cm) basswood and finished with boiled linseed oil. The patterns for these projects can be found on pages 202 and 203.

Both sugar and tea were precious commodities in the English kitchen. Special spoons or scoops were carved to carefully measure each leaf and grain. This *English Honeycomb Braid Sugar Scoop* has a four-line knot pattern around the handle and a smaller cameo knot inside the scoop. Carved from a 2" x 2" x 12" (5 x 5 x 30 cm) basswood blank, the finished scoop was decorated by woodburning the knot patterns. The patterns for this project can be found on pages 95 and 127.

This *Leaf-Tailed Dragon* would be a perfect accent for a young lady's jewelry box or hope chest. Woodburned on birch plywood, the design also includes a little lettering to personalize the burning. Notice how easy it is to add a small knot to the lettering to give the name a Celtic look. The Mammen stage of Celtic art introduced organic elements, such as this dragon's leaf tail. The pattern for this project can be found on page 151.

This premanufactured wooden clock's face became a wonderful canvas for *Time's A-Wasting*, a woodburned circular knot design with *Laced Lovebirds* as the center accent. A small touch of watercolor work was added to enhance the circular aspects of the pattern. Gripping beasts were a favorite theme during the Oseberg/Broa stage of Viking/Celtic artwork. The pattern for this project can be found on page 198.

Religious crosses, such as this *Celtic Cross 2*, are popular patterns in today's Celtic art. Though this project was created by woodburning a birch plywood blank, it would be as beautiful carved, scroll sawn, or even stitched as an appliqué quilt top. The pattern for this project can be found on page 207.

Flaunt your Celtic style by adding art to a t-shirt! Trace or draw a pattern onto a plain shirt. Use a black fabric marker to define the pattern better and then add color to make it vibrant. A variety of dragon and other animal patterns can be found on pages 144–169.

The Viking influence on Celtic art is clearly shown in this Viking king shirt. Much of the first block-out coats of white acrylic were allowed to show through the final coloring of this *Viking King and Horse Panel*. Because the cotton fabric of this shirt is lightweight, I first stretched the back of the shirt over several thicknesses of cardboard and secured the area with straight pins. After the design was completed, I thinned each of the colors that I used in the painting with water and splattered the entire area using a toothbrush. I set the color by soaking a tea towel in vinegar water, laying that towel over the color area, and ironing until the towel was dry. The pattern for this project can be found on page 190.

Celtic knot designs lend themselves easily to stencil work and block cuts. For this *Brocade Birdcage* linoleum block, the pattern was traced using carbon paper. The outlines of the tracing were cut first to create the stencil image. Then, the background area was removed to create a positive print. Jelling stage animals can use their tails, necks, legs, and bodies as part of the interlocked line designs. The pattern for this project can be found on page 158.

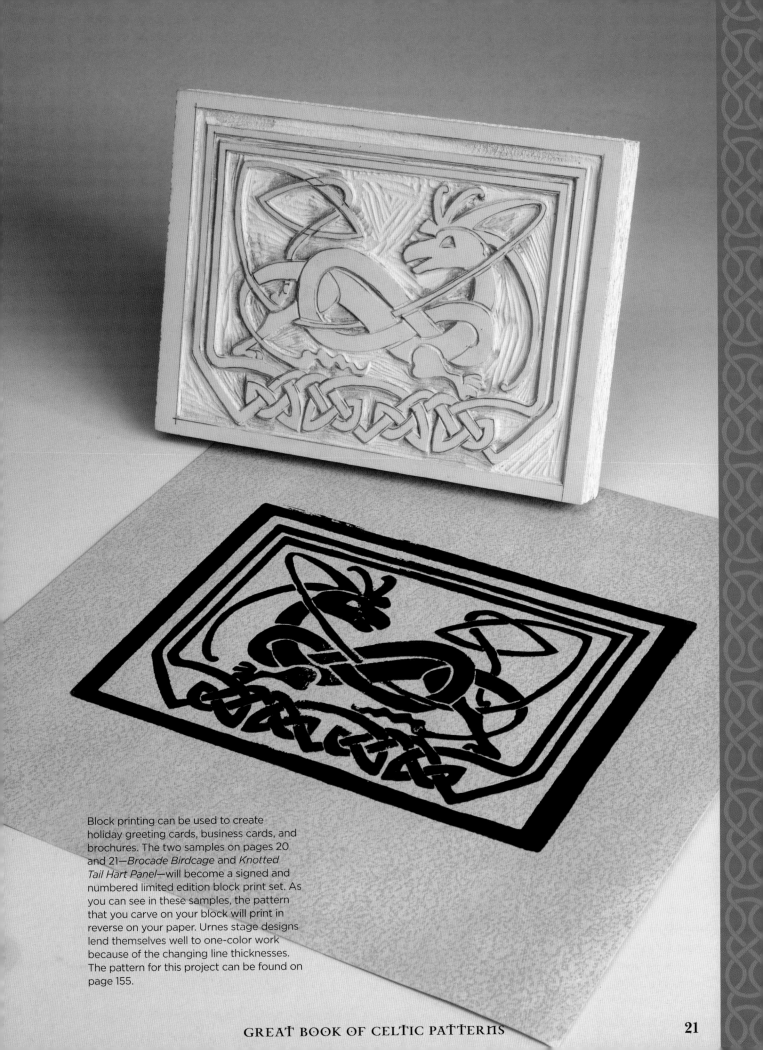

Block printing can be used to create holiday greeting cards, business cards, and brochures. The two samples on pages 20 and 21—*Brocade Birdcage* and *Knotted Tail Hart Panel*—will become a signed and numbered limited edition block print set. As you can see in these samples, the pattern that you carve on your block will print in reverse on your paper. Urnes stage designs lend themselves well to one-color work because of the changing line thicknesses. The pattern for this project can be found on page 155.

This leather binder is
beautifully decorated with
a corner Viking bird design.
This pattern can be found
on page 147.

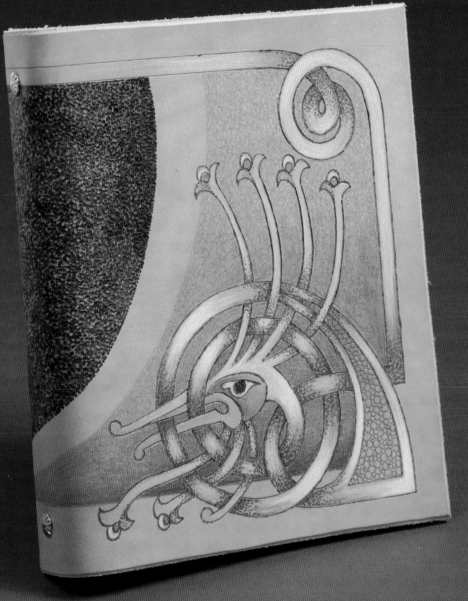

The outside of your scrapbook can be just as creative as the inside pages. This intricate dragon design has pale watercolor accents, as well as splattered colors all around to add interest. A toothbrush dipped in a watercolor and then flicked onto the leather created the effect. This pattern can be found on page 143.

Utility and artistry combine in this handy tote bag. First, I created a large quilted square with a bright border, colorful squares, and a colored Viking horse on the center white block. This quilted piece, slightly smaller than the bag, was then sewn to the bag on three sides. The top is open, creating a useful pocket for more storage space. The pattern for this project can be found on page 162.

Instead of small squares creating the frame around this Viking bird, strips of colorful fabric were quilted on a square that fit on one side of a canvas tote bag. The top side of the quilted piece was not sewn, creating a large pocket. The pattern for this project can be found on page 160.

You can use carbon paper to trace the double horses pattern onto a blank, wooden wall plaque. The pattern was then darkened by woodburning and color added with watercolors to add depth. The pattern for this project can be found on page 140.

The intricate bird pattern woodburned onto this wood blank adds interest to an otherwise ordinary coat hanger. The rough edges with bark intact add to the rustic feel. Select a burnished metal hanger with complementary details to enhance the whole look. The pattern for this project can be found on page 160.

Create an inspirational piece of Celtic art to hang in your own home or give as a gift. This lion was colored with soft shades of green and brown, making the pops of orange really stand out and make this an eye-catching piece. This lion pattern can be found on page 164.

God grant me the Serenity

Vivid colors of paint bring this stork to life. This simple
wooden board could be framed as hanging art or
included in another crafting project. The pattern used
in this project can be found on page 166.

This quilt would look equally at home hanging on a wall as the focal point of the room or draped over your lap as you snuggle down to watch a movie. The colorful triangle quilt pattern makes the black and white Celtic blocks stand out.

This stork pattern can be found on page 166.

This bird pattern can be found on page 160.

This tree of life pattern can be found on page 180.

CHAPTER 3

Celtic Line and Knot Patterns

UNDERSTANDING TWISTS, BRAIDS, AND KNOTTED LINES

Interlacing and interlocking line designs come in a variety of twisted, braided, and knotted patterns, known as straight-line designs. The simplest type of straight-line design is a twist. Adding additional lines turns a twist into a braid. Other types of straight-line designs include stand-alone patterns, such as one-line knots and multiple-line knots. The most complicated types of straight-line design are tangle designs. In this chapter, we'll take a look at how to create each of these designs.

Repeating patterns in straight-line designs

Although some are complicated tangles of interlaced loops, most Celtic-style knot designs use a rhythmic repeating pattern to create the final line work. Those repeating patterns can easily be seen in straight-line designs. Celtic lines can also be made up of interlocking, self-contained knot patterns and inserted knot units. Free-flowing lines interlace whereas independent self-contained knots can interlock.

Within any Celtic knot, twist, braid, or tangle, the lines that create those knots follow an over-and-under pattern of weaving. Each line will cross over another line at an intersection. At the next intersection this same line comes to, it will be woven under the crossing line. So each line will go over one line, and then go under the next line. If the intersections of a line continue throughout the

design in this over-and-under pattern, that pattern is called a perfect weave.

For some patterns, because insertions have been added or because the knot pattern is used to frame an inner design, that over-and-under weaving pattern can be broken or disturbed. You will find several patterns in the pattern section where one line is forced over two or more intersections or forced under two or more intersections. These types of non-continuous woven designs are called imperfect weaves.

Discovering the repeated knot or interlock pattern will allow you to easily adapt that knot design to corners, circles, and free-flowing artwork in the following chapters. Let's take a closer look at each of these designs.

Twists

Twists are the simplest line designs for Celtic knot patterns and are created when two or more lines are laid one over the other to create an interlacing pattern (see **Figure 3.1** and **Figure 3.2**). Twist patterns always repeat the over-and-under rhythm.

A twist pattern is easily adapted to specific measurement needs in pattern work since each twist unit is identical to all other twists in the line. You can vary the height and width of the twists, and each pattern can contain several different height and width variations (see **Figure 3.3** and **Figure 3.4**). Several sets of two-line twists can be combined or laid over each other to create more complicated-looking designs (see **Figure 3.5** and **Figure 3.6**). Twisted line patterns, as with any Celtic knot design, can use both curved sides and angled sides (see **Figure 3.7**). Twists are perfect for straight edges, curved or circular designs, and curved corners. Simply add or subtract twists from

a twisted line pattern to adjust that pattern to fit your particular project requirements. By dropping a twist, you decrease the length of the line pattern. If you add twists, you increase the length of the design (see **Figure 3.8**).

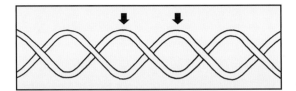

Figure 3.1. Two lines twisted one across the other over an even spacing creates the most basic of interlocking line patterns. Notice how the top line always falls over the bottom line or, in other words, how the left line always crosses over the right line.

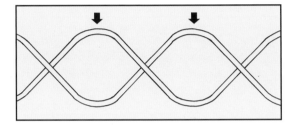

Figure 3.2. The size of the line pattern can be changed by widening the spacing or by widening the height of the curves within the twist, but the over-and-under rhythm of the line remains the same.

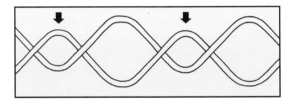

Figure 3.3. This line has a simple repeat of one large twist followed by one small twist, creating a rickrack look. Again, the over-and-under rhythm of the line remains.

Figure 3.4. The number of small and large twists within one line can be easily changed, making this pattern type extremely versatile.

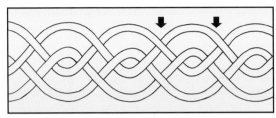

Figure 3.5. For this pattern, two sets of twisting lines have been interlaced. Each set contains the identical one-large-twist-and-one-small-twist pattern. Even in the four-line twist, the rhythm of the interlacing remains the same in every repeat of the pattern.

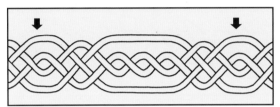

Figure 3.6. Here, the two sets of twisted lines are different from each other. The outer twist contains a one-large-twist-and-one-medium-twist pattern, while the inner twist is created with a three-small-twists-and-one-medium-twist pattern.

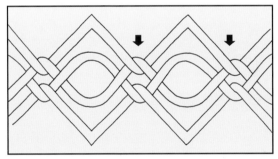

Figure 3.7. This pattern uses two sets of identical twist patterns. Each twist contains one curved side and one angled side to make the diamond edges.

Figure 3.8. This sample has three twists within one larger twist area. The number of times that you repeat the twist pattern determines the length of the line.

Braids

Interlacing three or more lines creates a braided pattern, which is slightly more complicated than a twist. Here are samples of basic three- (see **Figure 3.9**), four- (see **Figure 3.10**), and five-line (see **Figure 3.11**) braids. Usually, braids are worked with an evenly repeated spacing, but you can vary this spacing, as shown in **Figure 3.12** and **Figure 3.13**. Braids do not have to be created with the same size lines throughout, either. Braids are excellent design choices for borders, straight edges, curves, and corners and can be used to fill very large areas of pattern work in a lattice effect.

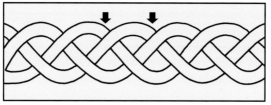

Figure 3.9. The three-line braid is the most basic interlocking line pattern.

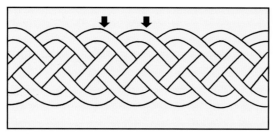

Figure 3.10. Working a braid with four lines adds an X pattern to the center of the braid.

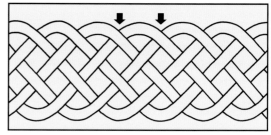

Figure 3.11. The five-line braid begins to take on the look of latticework. The more lines you add to a braid, the larger the center of the latticework becomes.

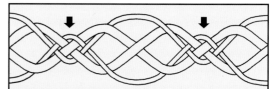

Figure 3.12. This pattern uses one pair of thin lines in contrast to the second pair of thick lines. Even though it follows the four-line braid weave, by changing the size of the loops in different areas, the overall look of the braid is altered.

Figure 3.13. Twist and braid patterns can vary in the number of lines used, in the size of each loop area used, and even in the thickness of the lines that are interlaced.

Knotted lines

Once you've mastered twists and braids, knotted lines are your next challenge. When making knots, the line turns back upon itself to create the interlacing. Knots can be created using only one line or using multiple lines, and they can be as simple as one loop or as complex as multiple loops that become tangles.

If you wish to completely fill an area or move from one design pattern into another, the knotted line is an excellent choice. Let's take a look at the three types of knotted lines: one-line knots, multiple-line knots, and tangles.

One-Line Knots

The one-line knot pattern is a common theme in Celtic work. It can be as simple as a one-line twist (see **Figure 3.14**). The look of the knotted line can be quickly changed by adjusting the shape of the loops and by adding angles within the loops for variety (see **Figure 3.15** and **Figure 3.16**). You can thread the line through the loops of a knot as many times as you wish to create larger knot patterns (see **Figure 3.17**). Very simple looped knots can often create beautiful repeated patterns that flow throughout the artwork (see **Figure 3.18**).

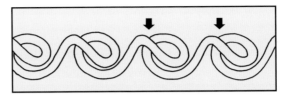

Figure 3.14. This simple knot pattern turns back upon itself in one loop, still repeating its over-and-under rhythm throughout the line. You can see that the upper line of the loop always lies over the curved area of the loop.

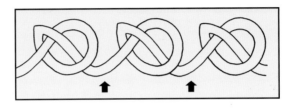

Figure 3.15. For this sample, the line creates a loop, as in Figure 3.14, but then is threaded through the opening made by that loop. This is a half-hitch knot.

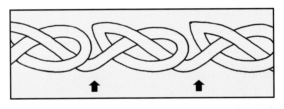

Figure 3.16. In this pattern, the knot has been stretched to make a long knot, plus one of the loops is angled while the other retains a curved profile.

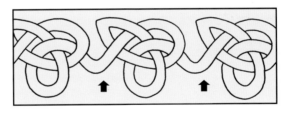

Figure 3.17. Even though this knot interlaces three times through its loops, the over-and-under rhythm remains the same in all of the knots.

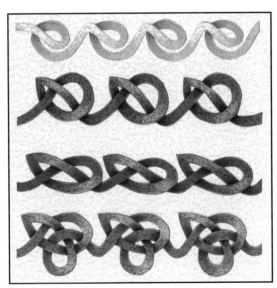

Figure 3.18. Because these samples use simple knots, your eye can quickly follow the over-and-under rhythm that leads into the next knot.

Multiple-Line Knots

Line knots can also be created using multiple lines. In a two-line simple knot pattern, the size of any loop within a knot can be adjusted to make room for new interlaced lines. These multiple lines can follow either identical patterns (see **Figure 3.19** and **Figure 3.20**) or varied patterns (see **Figure 3.21**) to complete the finished knot.

Tangles

So far, the patterns in this chapter have featured repeated patterns, which were created with lines that cross over once then continue on to a new knot or twist. Tangles, however, twist, turn, and fold upon themselves without any predictable pattern and can turn back into the knot multiple times (see **Figure 3.22** and **Figure 3.23**), making them the most difficult type of knotted-line work. Tangles are perfect for filling in large areas of work or for enhancing motifs such as animals (see **Figure 3.24**).

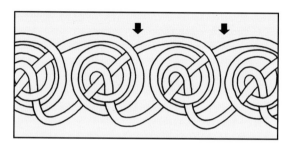

Figure 3.19. The two-line simple knot pattern is made using the two identical, simple loop knot lines. The end of one line is then threaded or interlaced through the loop of the second line.

Figure 3.20. This is a variation of Figure 3.19. The lines create a spiral look by adding circles around the basic loop. Two identical lines are used to make this design.

Figure 3.21. This Viking King and Horse Panel shows a multiple-line design created with varying knot patterns.

Figure 3.22. This pattern sample is made up of three identical tangles. Within the actual knot pattern, the line turns and interlaces itself over and over again until the knot area has been filled.

Figure 3.23. The shaded version of this knot pattern shows both the under and over interlacing of the pattern as well as how the knot is repeated to create the final line.

Figure 3.24. This Viking animal sample shows how a tangle knot can be used to fill the space of a design. The tangle is created using four interlaced lines. One line is the basic spiral knot created by the dragon's body. That body spiral interlocks with a two-line mirror-image knot. The fourth tangle line is from the elongated muzzle and also laces with the two-line mirror-image knot.

Inserted units

Some Celtic knot patterns have inserted units that are self-contained. These inserts enhance a simple twist, braid, or knot pattern. Circles (see **Figure 3.25**), figure eights, and diamonds are some commonly inserted units. Inserted units can be used at every intersection to enhance a corner or central point in the line.

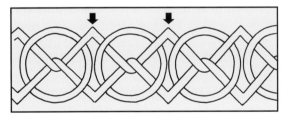

Figure 3.25. This pattern is a simple twist design using two lines. A circle design has been added at the intersections of the twist.

Interlocking units

Just as self-contained units can be added to a line design, several self-contained units can be interlocked to create the knotting pattern of a line. With interlocking knots (see **Figure 3.26**), each knot is woven into the knot behind it and the knot ahead of it to continue the line movement.

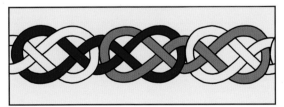

Figure 3.26. This pattern is created by interlocking one self-contained unit with another. Each unit connects to one unit on one side and another unit on the other side. Repeating this pattern keeps the line growing.

CHAPTER 4

Plotting and Graphing Knots

USING GRAPH PAPER TO CREATE AND MODIFY KNOTTED LINES

Graphing or plotting a knotted line is the easiest way to create new layouts and new knot patterns. To plot a line pattern, you will need graph paper, colored pencils, and an eraser. The scale of the graph paper, from four squares to the inch to ten squares to the inch, acts as a guide to the size and thickness of your knotted line. Using graph paper with fewer squares per inch will give you a large and thick knot. The more squares per inch, the smaller and thinner your knot will be. Let's take a closer look.

SUPPLY LIST

- ☐ Graph paper, or a photocopy of the provided sheets
- ☐ Colored pencils
- ☐ Eraser

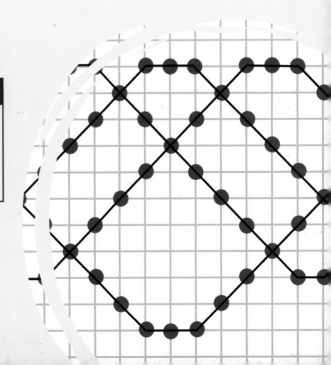

Exercise 1: Plotting a simple knot pattern

This is a simple half-hitch knot pattern that creates a heart shape. To create the pattern, graph out and connect the lines, as shown in the demonstration below.

1 Start at one end of the thread, and notice how the over-and-under pattern that we saw throughout Chapter 3 is repeated here.

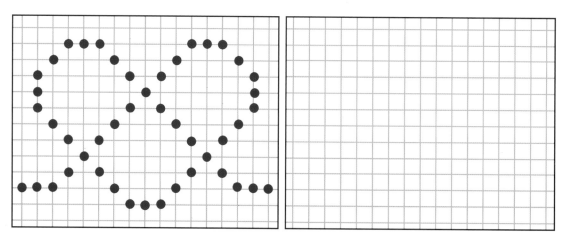

2 With a colored pencil, mark where the knot will touch the intersections of the graph squares. Note how the graph paper can guide you in creating both straight and diagonal lines. The first pencil plotting will have angular corners. These will become curved later in the graph work.

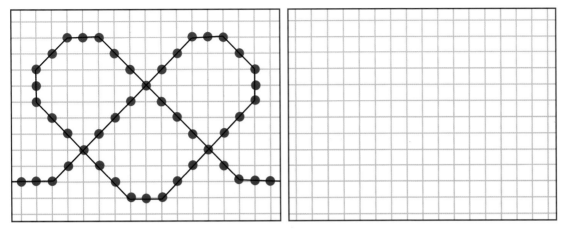

3 Once the knot has been plotted, connect the dots with a pencil line.

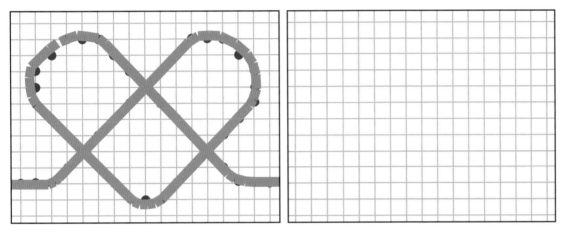

4 Widen the pencil line to the desired thickness by drawing lines on either side of the original line. As you establish the thickness of the line, also smooth out the curves in the loops.

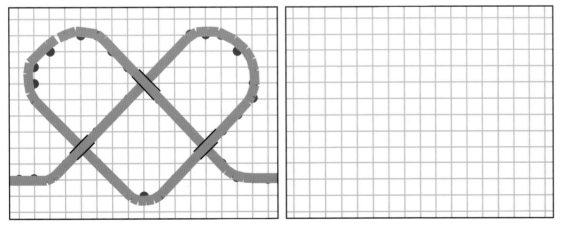

5 Place your finger on one end of the knotted line. Follow the line up to the first intersection of your knot. With a pencil, mark the line as lying on top of or over the intersected line. Move your finger along the same line to the next intersection. Here, mark the line as going beneath or under the second line. Continue marking the intersections in an over-and-under pattern until the entire knot has been worked.

Exercise 2: Creating a new pattern from a plotted pattern

Now that you have created a half-hitch knot, let's alter it to make it a self-contained knot by looping the lines back through the design and joining them together.

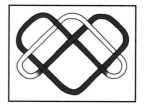

1 Study the pattern. You can see the basic heart-shaped knot shown in Step 1 of Exercise 1 within this new pattern. In the previous exercise, the knot ended with straight lines. For this pattern, those lines will be looped back into the knot to join at the top of the heart. If you trace your finger along the path of the knot, you'll notice that the over-and-under pattern is still present.

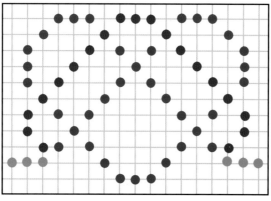
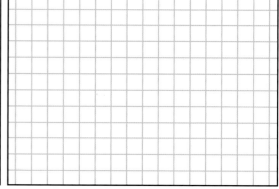

2 Plot the original heart-shaped knot pattern in red ink. Here, I've marked the ends of the lines at the bottom of the heart knot in gold. These gold plot marks will not be used in the new knot. The blue plot marks show where the end lines loop back into the knot to join at the top of the heart.

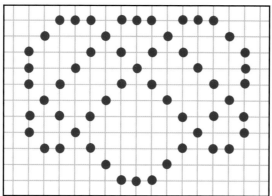
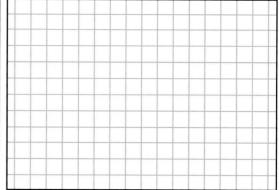

3 Here is the new pattern plotted out.

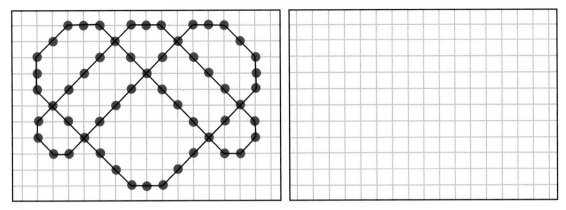

4 Use a pencil to draw a guideline connecting all of the plot marks.

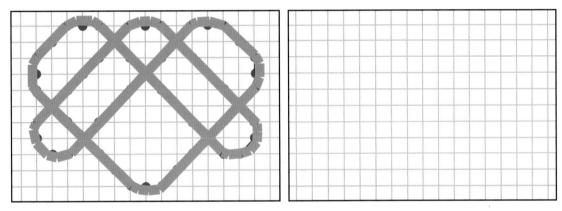

5 Widen the guideline to the final thickness of the knotted line.

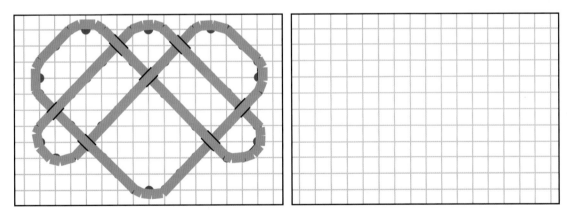

6 Place your finger on one area of the line. Move your finger along that line, marking each intersection as an over or under junction.

Exercise 3: Creating more complicated patterns from plotted designs

As you become more at ease with plotting Celtic knots, you will begin to work more complicated designs from the patterns in this book. Breaking a line into two segments then lengthening those new segments is a simple way to give your pattern more depth.

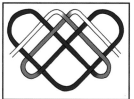

1 Study the pattern. This one is worked from the knot we just finished in Exercise 2, and you can still see the simple heart pattern knot from Exercise 1 that both knots are based on.

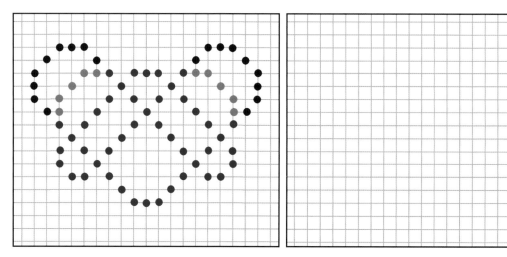

2 Using red, draw the plot marks that will be incorporated from Step 3 of Exercise 2. Because this new pattern will need space for the additional lines inside the loops of the heart, the original loops (gold plot marks) have been changed. Draw the larger loop in blue plotting marks. The gold plotting marks will not be used in the new design.

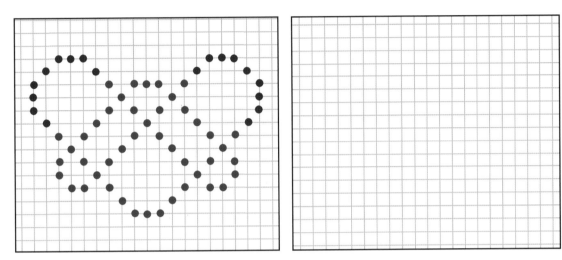

3 Here are the plot marks for the new knot up to this point. You can make the loops as large as necessary to create room for as many new interlocking lines as you like. Here, I'll be adding just one additional line.

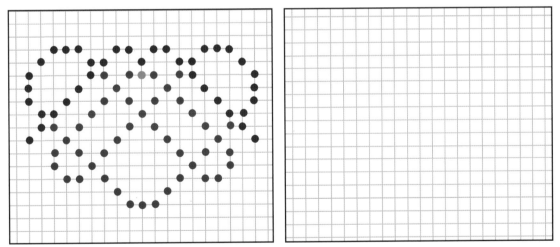

4 Extend and cross the original interlocking lines that run through the center of the heart, shown in red, to break the line into two places. Use blue plot marks to show where these lines will cross in between the two loops then fold back down into the loop areas above the original interlocking lines. The gold plot mark will not be used in the new design.

Exercise 3: Creating more complicated patterns from plotted designs *(continued)*

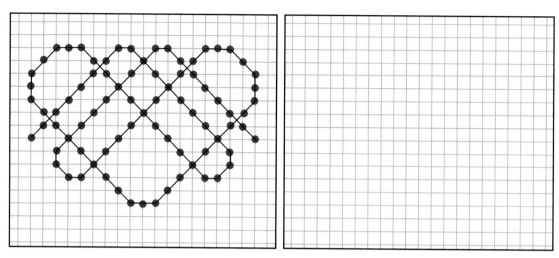

5 Add a pencil line to connect the plot marks. You can see the two new lines inside the upper sections of the loops.

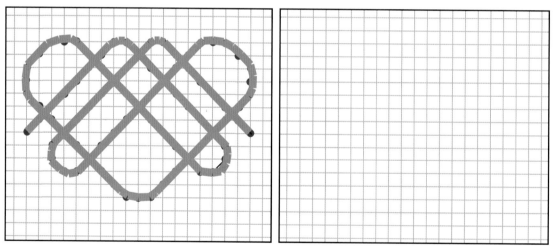

6 Widen your guideline to the correct thickness for your knot.

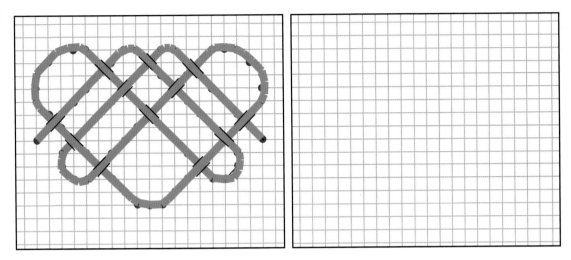

7 Place your finger on one end of the knot. Follow along the line, marking each
intersection as an over or under junction.

Exercise 4: Breaking a knot pattern into multiple lines

New loops and turns are not the only elements you can add to a plotted pattern.

You can also break the pattern lines into new sections to create multiple-line patterns.

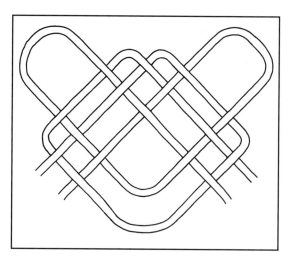

1 Study the pattern. Again, this pattern is worked from the previously plotted pattern for Exercise 3. The new pattern contains two lines.
One line is very similar to the original heart pattern in Exercise 1.
It is interlocked with a second line that encircles the heart.

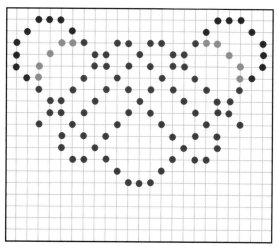
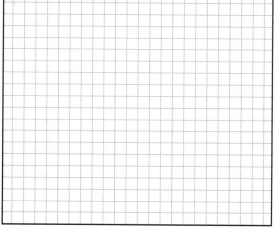

2 Begin by plotting out the pattern from Step 5 of Exercise 3, shown in red plot marks. The loops of the original heart shape are marked in gold and will not be used in the new pattern. Widen the loops to allow room for the new intersection lines, shown in blue.

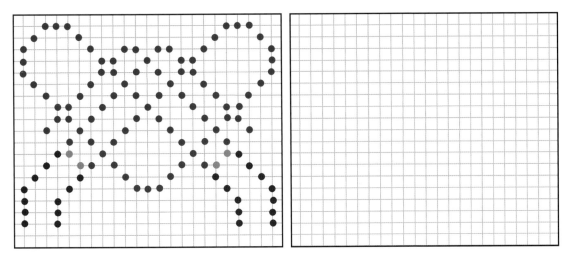

3 Break the bottom tight loops into two individual lines. The new plot marks are shown in blue; the old plot marks in gold.

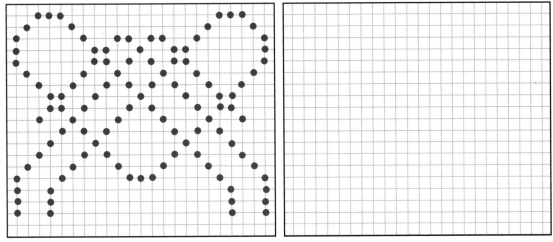

4 Your new design should have three open-ended lines on each side of the heart area.

Exercise 4: Breaking a knot pattern into multiple lines *(continued)*

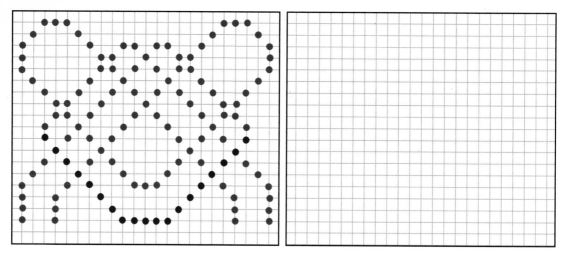

5 Connect the upper open-ended lines to each other by plotting a large loop below the heart area, as shown in blue.

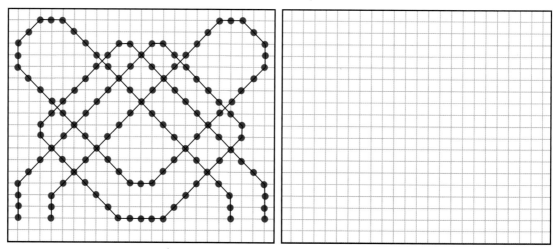

6 Draw a pencil line between the plot marks to connect the dots.

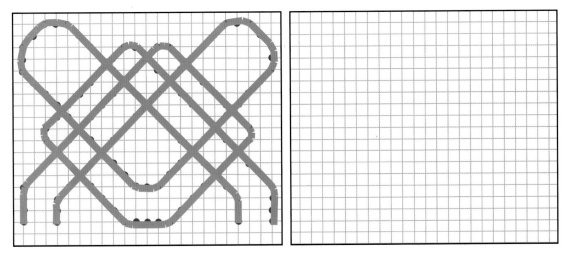

7 Widen the guideline to the thickness you want for your finished knot.

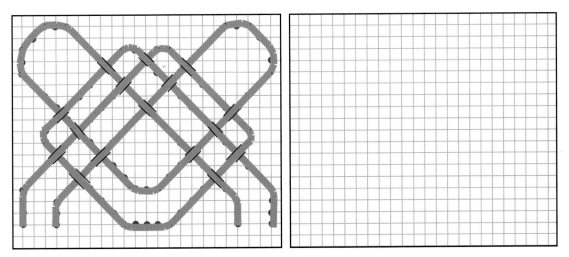

8 Place your finger on one end of the knot. Follow that line, marking each intersection as an over or under junction. Because this pattern is created using two separate lines, you will need to repeat this step for the second line, continuing the over-and-under layout for each junction point.

The next steps

Any type of Celtic twist, braid, or knot can be plotted and altered in the same manner. If you would like to practice on some designs, try plotting the illustrations in Chapter 3 and then altering them.

Once your knot is plotted, you'll want to trace it onto plain paper. After you have become familiar with the process of graphing Celtic designs, you may also want to try out one of the drawing or Celtic knot computer programs that are available. These may help speed up the process. Your final illustration should show all of the over-and-under intersections clearly, similar to the final step in each of the exercises shown here.

CHAPTER 5

Layout Ideas

Once you have created a knot pattern, it's time to place that pattern in a layout for your design work. Interlaced and interlocked patterns are easily adapted and can be used for any design area, including line work, corners, circles, and cameo motifs. This section will explore a few of the basic layouts used with knot patterns and lines.

Basic layouts

The half-hitch pattern, or heart, that we plotted in Exercise 1 in Chapter 4 is an excellent knot sample to show how layouts can be arranged. Two or more hearts can be strung together side-by-side (see **Figure 5.1**), or they can be intertwined (see **Figure 5.2**). A self-contained knot can easily be placed in the corners or along the sides of a square (see **Figure 5.3**). By orienting the hearts to different positions, other complex designs can be created (see **Figure 5.4** to **Figure 5.5**).

Figure 5.1. In this sample, the heart knot has been connected to create a straight-line pattern with each knot standing alone.

Figure 5.2. Here, the loops of one heart interlace with the loops of the next heart knot. This pattern connects multiple knots with new intersections.

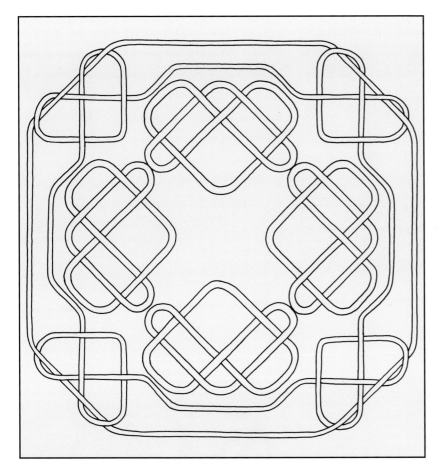

Figure 5.3. In this sample, the center knots are allowed to touch, which strengthens the square feeling of the layout. The heart knots along the outer edge are placed in the corners and are connected to become one line. An outer line that weaves over and under the loops of the heart was added to finish the square feeling of this pattern.

Figure 5.5. Patterns with open lines can easily be mirrored and connected to become one large pattern.

Figure 5.4. If you are working with one knot pattern but want a varied or wavy look to your line, try reversing the knots. Laying out the knots in a one-up-and-one-down pattern adds interest to the final design.

Corner ideas

Line designs will need to be adjusted when they are used around the corner of a square or rectangular layout pattern, and using a different knot pattern in the corner gives greater emphasis to that corner area.

Several visually interesting options are available for corners. One option is to create a corner by overlapping two one-line designs that end in finials (see **Figure 5.6**). A second option is to interlock two independent line patterns (see **Figure 5.7**). If your design incorporates braids, the braids can be woven together to create one self-contained corner pattern (see **Figure 5.8**). A final option includes the use of newly created knot patterns that are simply placed over the corners (see **Figure 5.9** and **Figure 5.10**). Corner motifs can be placed directly over the adjoining knot lines so that the lines disappear under that motif.

As you've seen in this chapter, not all knot patterns are self-contained, meaning that not all knots are created from one continuous, connected line. Celtic knot patterns and lines can use finials, can have added decorations on a line, and can have stopped or broken lines.

Figure 5.6. This corner is created using two one-line designs. Each line has a finial, which is an added decoration on a line to stop or break that line. The finials are allowed to simply overlap at the corner intersection.

Figure 5.7. In this sample, the corner is also created from two independent line patterns. The open loop at the end of one line is allowed to overlap and there interlock with the loop of the second line.

Figure 5.8. A four-line braid pattern makes up this corner idea. Two of the lines from the braid are moved through the corner area and into the braid on the other side. The corner has a simple overlap pattern as the transition point. With the use of the corner lines, these two braided side sections have become one self-contained corner pattern.

Figure 5.10. Square motifs can be easily added to a corner joint where two lines meet. Adding a square motif eliminates the problem of creating a new knot pattern in the corner area and creates a focal point within the design.

Figure 5.9. Because this corner is created from a one-line knot pattern, it is easy to insert a new and different one-line knot for the corner transition.

CHAPTER 6

Pattern Changes

Because there are no rules in Celtic knot work, other than the over-and-under pattern of intersections, knotted line patterns can easily be changed or adjusted to fit within the space requirements of your craft or art. Splits, points, and insertions are just a few of the tricks that can be employed to alter Celtic knots to fit any scenario. Each of these changes is equally easy to accomplish, and several can be used together to create a new design.

Splitting the line

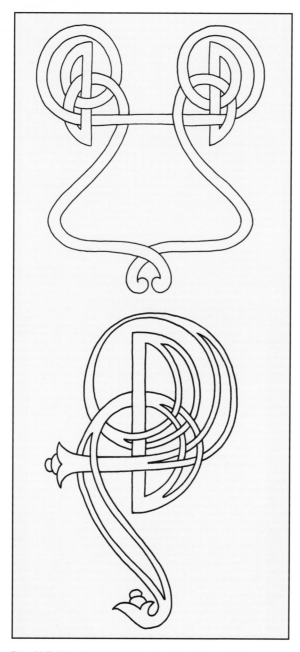

The lines within a Celtic knot pattern can be split or divided at any place inside the knot. These split sections can follow the original line's over-and-under lacing pattern, or they can become new lines that interlock independently from the original line (see **Figure 6.1**). Split lines can even join other split lines to create new loops within the knot (see **Figure 6.2**).

Adding split sections to your knot pattern creates more over-and-under work within the lacing. It also gives variety to the line work within the knot because some of the lines will be thick in comparison to the thinner split lines.

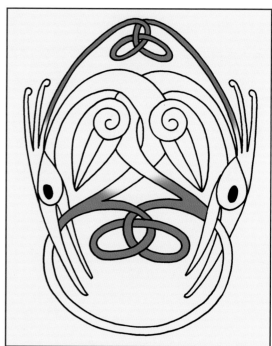

Figure 6.1. The D-ring knot pattern (top) employs a line of the same thickness throughout the design. It has a simple and easy-to-follow interlacing. The bottom sample is based on the above D-ring knot pattern. In the new design, the right-hand side of each curve in the knot has been split into two pieces. Each part of the split line has then been allowed to interlace. The very simple knot from the D-ring pattern now has a complex look. The use of thick and thin line areas in the design emphasizes the wide vertical and horizontal crossed lines.

Figure 6.2. The body of this double bird pattern splits at the top of the circular loop, one split line per side. Those two split lines then join within the loop to create a knot inside the circle area. The long scroll feathers at the top of the design also join to become a knot pattern. This design shows the use of thick and thin lines, with the body area being the widest portion of the line and the split knots becoming the thinnest.

Adding angles and points to fill your space

Adding angles and points to a curved design also lends interest to the work. In an otherwise curved and flowing pattern, the occasional point pulls the eye to that area of the knot design (see **Figure 6.3**).

Figure 6.3. This is a two-line pattern that has open areas between the knotted sections of the line. Angles have been used to emphasize the triangle shape within the main knot.

Adding inserted units

Inserted units can be added to fill in an otherwise open, lacy design (see **Figure 6.4**). Squares, diamonds, circles, and heart designs are simple inserts that can add interest to a knotted line design. Figure-eight designs and self-contained knot designs can also be used to create a more complicated look.

Figure 6.4. A heart-shaped insert unit has been added to fill the spaces between the original knotted line design. The point of the heart has been placed to match the points created in the original loop. The pattern now has a solid feeling to it.

Adding spiral turns

Twisting spirals that continue the over-and-under pattern of the knot can quickly and easily fill out any open space in a knot pattern (see **Figure 6.5**).

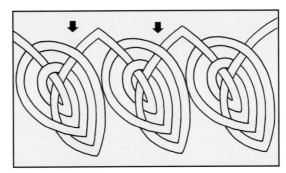

Figure 6.5. These new loops can be circular or pointed or some of both, as shown here, depending on the area that you need to fill.

Stretching the lines and loops

Angles and points can be added in the loop areas to bring the design down to touch the outline of another area. Loops can be pulled and stretched to give added length to your pattern (see **Figure 6.6**).

Figure 6.6. Loops can be pulled and stretched to fill open areas in a design. Here, one of the lower loops has been pulled toward the center of the knot pattern and has been sharply pointed to fill the space.

CHAPTER 7

Finials for Interlocking Designs

USING ANIMALS, LEAVES, AND SCROLLS TO FINISH KNOTTED LINES

Adding finials, the ornamental elements that cap open lines, is a great way to add interest to your Celtic knot work. In addition to completing any open lines in your designs, finials can establish the style of a design through the use of historical elements, such as Viking animals and Romanesque leaves, or other embellishments, such as scrolls and flowers. And, because interlocking line designs are used in so many art styles and throughout many historical periods, the variety of finials is wide open to your imagination. You may even decide to break some of the lines in your knot work to allow for the addition of finials. In this chapter, we'll take a closer look at the various types of finials that cover the end of a line.

How to add finials to your designs

Figure 7.1. This Celtic knot pattern has two open-ended lines that can be adapted to create a Viking animal design using finials.

Let's take a look at some examples of ways to add finials to your Celtic knots. The most common ways to add finials is to add them to a knot with open-ended lines or to break a knot to create open-ended lines for your finials.

Figure 7.1 shows a simple, open-ended knot that is a perfect candidate for the addition of finials. In **Figure 7.2**, I've added stylized animal heads to the open line areas. Notice how all of the elements keep the weaving pattern of the design.

Figure 7.3 shows a self-contained knot that can be adapted to allow for finials by breaking a line to create two open ends. **Figure 7.4** illustrates how the finials were added to the broken line.

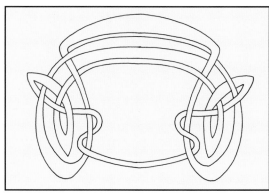

Figure 7.3. This self-contained line pattern can be adapted to accept finials by breaking one line to create the open ends that are needed to accept the animal heads.

Figure 7.2. Stylized animal heads have been added to the open lines of the knot in Figure 7.9. Notice how the head scroll lines interlace with the knot and the mouths and tongues also interlock. These particular animals have three scroll lines coming from their heads. The longest scroll line, the one on the outer edge of the pattern, laces twice through one loop of the original knot pattern. The two smaller ones lace as a set with one over the original loop and the next under the original loop, keeping the rhythm of the knot.

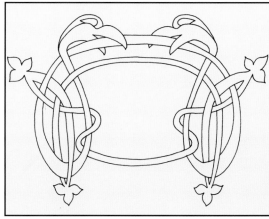

Figure 7.4. Here, the top arched line of Figure 7.3 has been broken to allow for the addition of this pair of stylized bird heads. Notice how the birds grasp the knot line below. Leaf-styled feet have been added to the angled loops of the original knot.

Whenever you add finials to your work, you'll find that it's best to do so in pairs, even if they have the illusion of being a single unit, to keep with the weaving pattern of your design. A one-line design, for example, can easily be changed into a Viking animal with a twisted tail and entwined neck (see **Figure 7.5**), a briar rose with interlocked stem and leaves, or even a classic Romanesque acanthus leaf design. Your finials can also be two distinct units, such as two animal heads (see **Figure 7.6**). Adding two interlacing areas from a finial is a way to enhance this effect. This means that one area will become the "over" part and the other area will become the "under" part that keeps the rhythm of your knot design (see **Figure 7.7**).

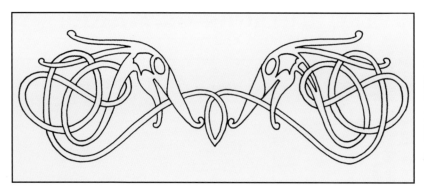

Figure 7.6. This knot features two very distinct animal heads as finials. Notice how they are incorporated into the weaving pattern of the design.

Figure 7.5. In this design, the knot pattern is also the animal's body, legs, and tail. Though the animal makes the design feel like a single unit, the head and the tail serve as the two finials capping the ends of the knot. This particular design contains an inserted figure-eight unit that adds more dimension to the piece.

Figure 7.7. Celtic knots can be windows or frames for Viking animals. This knotted pattern contains a large open circle. The space within that circle can be filled with any design or pattern. The two head scroll finials keep the rhythm of the original frame knot. The tail feathers are split to retain the over-and-under weaving pattern when crossing the circle.

Viking animals as finials

Figure 7.8. The top row shows the classic Viking deer design. Deer antlers are often shown as curved scroll lines. The second row shows the Viking horse, and the bottom row shows the snake pattern. This snake head can also appear as a bird's head if feathers are added as a topknot.

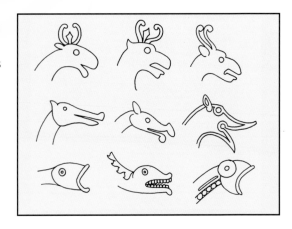

Viking animals of all sorts make interesting finials. Because the animals are so stylized, it is often hard to determine exactly what species an animal represents. **Figure 7.8** to **Figure 7.10** show examples of what artists have come to call deer, dogs, and birds. **Figure 7.11** shows some of the different ways to stylize your animals' feet and tails. Legs in these designs tend to appear as if they were attached to the animal's body as a separate piece, and that attachment point can happen anywhere within the knot design. As you can see in **Figure 7.11**, feet can be anything from a very simple hoof design to twisted and curved toes. Some feet even appear to become leaf patterns. Tails are important parts of Viking animal patterns because they can easily be lengthened or stretched to interlock with the original knot (see **Figure 7.12**). Additionally, Viking animals have no rules regarding where heads, legs, bodies, or tails fall within a pattern. Any of the loops in the original knot can be used to create any variety of body parts.

Figure 7.9. Dogs and wolves are very common images found in Viking animal patterns. As this image evolved, it took on exaggerated teeth and elongated muzzles. Some dog and wolf patterns become so exaggerated that they take on the appearance of wingless dragons.

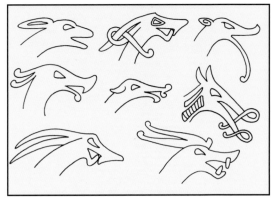

Figure 7.10. Birds were a favorite Viking image. Their beaks can be stretched to clasp the knotted line, and their topknots are often clusters of scroll lines that tangle with the knot pattern.

Figure 7.11. A wide variety of leg, feet, and tail designs go with the Viking animal heads.

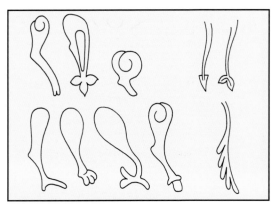

Figure 7.12. Notice how the tail is lengthened and how it is the only element of this Viking deer pattern that twists and interlocks. This keeps the deer as a recognizable image yet still has the fun of the over-and-under weave pattern found in Celtic knots.

Other styles of finials

Aside from Viking animals, many possible finials can be added to any knotted line pattern. Here are just a few ideas to get your imagination going. **Figure 7.13** and **Figure 7.14** show a variety of organic and geometric shapes that you can use in your finials.

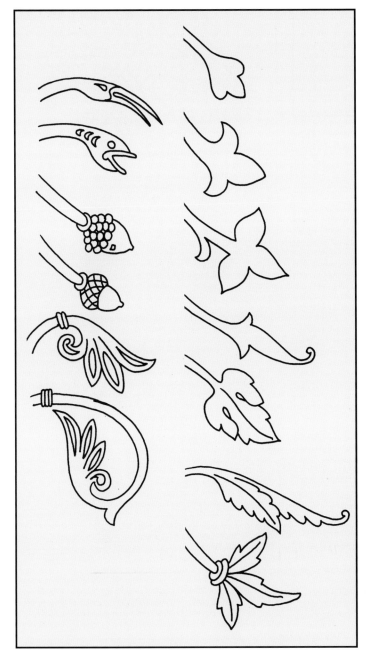

Figure 7.13. Leaves, flowers, and other organic materials create a lighter finished effect and give the overall design a beautiful flair.

Figure 7.14. Geometric finials add a crisp finish to a line.

Figure 7.15. This self-contained twist pattern would make a wonderful accent point to any craftwork and can be easily modified to accommodate finials.

Let's look at a variety of ways finials can enhance your designs. Breaking a self-contained knot allows for the addition of scrolls or more complex designs (see **Figure 7.15** to **Figure 7.17**).

Figure 7.17. Here, the knot from Figure 7.15 has been transformed into a Romanesque-style design. Leaves have been added as finials and incorporated into the interlocking pattern.

Figure 7.16. Breaking the knot from Figure 7.15 at the top loop allows for the addition of a simple scroll finial. These scrolls could now be interlaced with another knot pattern, a straight accent line, or even a monogram letter.

Simple, self-contained mirror image knots (where the top part of the knot is identical to the lower part of the knot) can provide an excellent starting point for adding finials (see **Figure 7.18** to **Figure 7.20**).

Figure 7.20. For this sample, the leaf pattern from Figure 7.19 has been changed from a stylized leaf into a realistic leaf design. Notice how the tips of the leaves have been elongated to interlace with the leaf stems. These leaves can be found in Italian Renaissance panels and friezes.

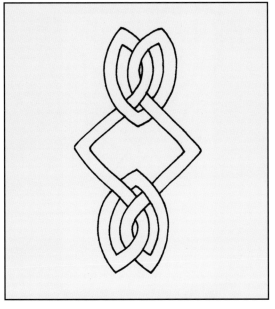

Figure 7.18. This self-contained mirror image knot can be easily broken to include finials.

Figure 7.19. The knot pattern in Figure 7.18 has been broken at the center to retain one half of the original pattern. A Viking/Celtic leaf design was added to the open-ended lines.

Recognizable symbols can make great finials and can change the appearance of a design dramatically. In **Figure 7.21** to **Figure 7.23**, a simple knot was used to create a bird-catching-a-fish knot and an Irish thistle knot.

Figure 7.21. This simple pattern is a good starting point for creating knots with symbols.

Figure 7.22. Here, the top line has been broken and animal heads have been added. The original pattern from Figure 7.21 has gone from a simple knot to a bird-catching-a-fish pattern.

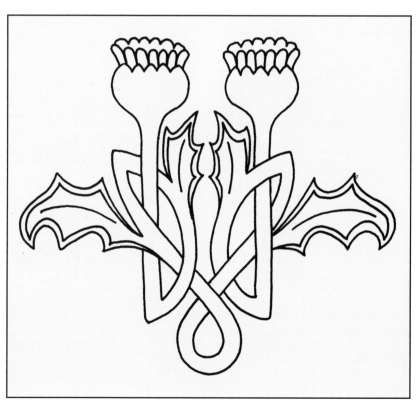

Figure 7.23. Classic Irish thistles were used here to create the finials for the knot pattern from Figure 7.21. The thistle flower is a good luck symbol for the Irish culture.

Larger knots, like the mirror image knot in **Figure 7.24**, can be modified to include finials, and these designs could fill a tabletop or chair back (see **Figure 7.25**). You can also retain only part of the mirror image for smaller options (see **Figure 7.26**).

Figure 7.25. Here, the knot from Figure 7.24 goes into a Gothic-styled leaf design. The leaf pattern seems to sit on top of the knot design as if it were a separate piece or unit.

Figure 7.24. This knot is a large mirror image pattern, which could fill a large area of work, such as a tabletop or chair back. It is perfect for working with finials.

Figure 7.26. The design from Figure 7.24 has been broken to retain one part of the mirror image. A small leaf flourish has been added.

Double knots are easily altered to become unique finials. I transformed the one in **Figure 7.27** into a Victorian design as an example (see **Figure 7.28**).

You can also keep any finials very simple so that the emphasis remains on the knot itself. **Figure 7.29** and **Figure 7.30** show two examples of simple but decorative finials.

Remember, the variations on finials and their placements are endless, and pairs of finials don't necessarily have to be the same size. As you develop your own, keep in mind the final use of the project. The elements of the finished piece may dictate how many and what types of finials should be used (see **Figure 7.31**).

Figure 7.27. This is a double knot pattern where one knot from one line section interlaces with the mirror image knot on the other line section. Breaking this type of pattern can create unique finials because of interlacing and rhythm.

Figure 7.28. The double knots in Figure 7.27 quickly became entwined branches for this Victorian berry pattern.

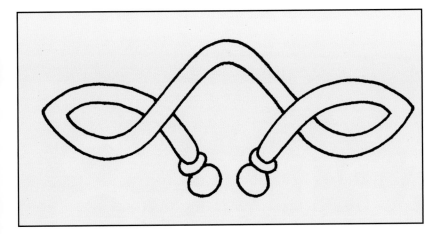

Figure 7.29. This simple twist design ends with a ball finial.

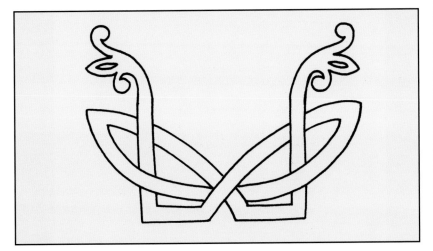

Figure 7.30. This butterfly knot ends with a three-piece scroll leaf finial that was common in Viking and Celtic work.

Figure 7.31. The same butterfly knot from Figure 7.30 appears in later Renaissance art as a doorplate accent. The top portion of the open-ended line has become a Green Man face (a face or figure that incorporates or is made of leaves, branches, or vines), and the bottom portion has been transformed into a finial to accent the doorplate's screw. Notice that the finials do not have to be the same size.

CHAPTER 8

Line Enhancements

How you treat the actual line within a knot can greatly change the way the pattern looks when it is finished. The line does not need to be a smooth, flowing line. It can become the body and legs of a Viking animal, the branches of a vine, or even a geometric pattern. Let's look at a few ideas on how to adjust the line within a knot pattern.

Texturing the pattern

The three-line-braid pattern appears in many historic styles of interlocking line patterns (see **Figure 8.1**). The lines in this pattern are smooth sided and without detail. Altering this line to create vines (see **Figure 8.2**) creates a more detailed look.

Just about any knot pattern can become a rope design (see **Figure 8.3**). The addition of leaves and flowers makes the design more complex (see **Figure 8.4**). These simple techniques will allow you to create any number of designs (see **Figure 8.5**).

Figure 8.1. Let's start with this example of a simple three-line braid pattern.

Figure 8.2. Here, each line of the same three-braid line from Figure 8.1 has become two stems of a vine. Each pair of vine stems interlock as if they were one unit; both go over then under the other pairs of stems in the design. Tendrils were added as accent pieces to the braided vines.

Figure 8.3. Notice that all of the rope pieces twist in the same direction, from top to bottom and left to right.

Figure 8.4. Three heavy branches make up this braid pattern. Leaf clusters and even flowered branches could be added as accent pieces.

Figure 8.5. Use this graph to practice the variations shown in this chapter and to create your own designs.

Adding space and geometric designs to patterns

In **Figure 8.6**, the lines of the original braid from Figure 8.1 have been broken in two. Because the thin lines do not have texture, the emphasis of this design is focused on the intersection points. Angles can also add interest to any knot design (see **Figure 8.7**).

A stencil design can be created by drawing a thin, open space in each line where an intersection occurs (see **Figure 8.8**), and patterns and textures can be added to any line in a knot design (see **Figure 8.9** and **Figure 8.10**).

The intersections of knots and the space between the loops of the pattern are perfect for accent images and texture work (see **Figure 8.11** to **Figure 8.12**).

Figure 8.6. Each line of the original braid has been broken into two thin lines for this pattern.

Figure 8.7. For this sample, each line becomes wider and angles along the outer curves of the braid then tapers to a thin spot where it intersects in the center of the braid.

Figure 8.8. The braid pattern now takes on the look of a brick design.

Figure 8.9. The simplest of designs can be transformed into very complex patterns. This heavy Gothic leaf accent uses a ball pattern within the line as well as a detailed pattern in the leaf areas.

Figure 8.10. This sample uses the same pattern for all three lines, but you can use different patterns for each line within the original knot.

Figure 8.11. Accent images can be used for the intersection areas of the knot pattern. This braid uses a small diamond design in the center interlaced areas.

Figure 8.12. Celtic knots capture space between the loops of the pattern. This space is perfect for accent images and texture work.

CHAPTER 9

Adding Color

A STEP-BY-STEP GUIDE TO ENHANCING YOUR WORK WITH COLOR

Many of the colored samples throughout this book have been created in artist's colored pencils. I enjoy this medium because of the flexibility it gives me as an artist and the vibrancy it creates. Unlike many other media, colored pencils require no water or cleaning media. You can easily sharpen them to the finest of points for very thin line work or use a wide or blunt point for easy fill work. By working the designs in very light layers of color, one over the other, on heavy weight, toothed paper or colored paper, your entire finished project can have a wide range of colors, tones, detailing, and texture. Using lots and lots of different colors is what gives the vibrancy to colored pencil work. Colored pencils are available in several styles, including artist-grade wax-based pencils, watercolor pencils, and oil pencils. Any of the three styles can be used for Celtic knot work designs. All of this means easy and quick fun in creating your own Celtic knot designs.

Using colored pencils

As I mentioned earlier, I used a heavy weight, 80-pound, colored, textured paper for the illustrations in this book. The coloring of the paper not only provides a colored background, but it can also become part of the shading and color mixing of the drawing. The texture of the paper gives a stone-carved feeling to the finished drawing. Colored pencils can also be used over many craft surfaces, including papier-mâché, pottery, and even woodburning.

Because colored pencils are translucent, allowing some light to show through, I like to start shading by using dark-toned pencil colors first. Over these dark tones, layers of brighter hues are added. Highlights can be added to an area with the use of top layers of light colors and white. New colors can also be created by this layering technique: a light yellow pencil color laid over a bright red will tint the red area to a shade of orange. A colored pencil drawing can easily have 20 to 40 layers of color applied (see **Figure 9.1**).

On the following pages, I'll show you step-by-step how to add color to your Celtic designs. We'll start with the darkest shading first and work our way through the final layer of color.

TIPS FOR WORKING WITH COLORED PENCILS

1 **Keep your pencils very sharp.**
Fine points create finely drawn lines.

2 **Lay down the color in very thin layers, and then develop the color by adding new thin layers.** The wax in colored pencils can build up quickly if the colored pencil is applied too heavily, and that thick wax layer will resist new colors being added.

3 **Using many different colors in one area enriches the look of a colored pencil drawing.** Experiment with the colors in your set to see which ones give you the best combinations. For example, you may develop a medium blue area by using dark reds and purples for the shading and pale greens or light grays for the highlights.

4 **Shading and highlights are often applied first.** Once these are applied, several light layers of a color can then be applied to the entire area. This will transform the shading and highlight colors into tones of the overall color.

5 **Mistakes with colored pencils can be easily corrected using clear tape.** First, gently lay tape over the area that you wish to remove. Do not press the tape down. Next, use an ink pen to mark the tape over just the area of color to be lifted. When you pick up the tape, it will pick up the colored pencil that was under the ink pen lines.

6 **Colored pencil work can be sealed with a spray sealer when the work is completed.** Spray sealer protects the drawing from dirt and dust buildup. I often use a reworkable spray sealer for my drawings. This type of spray protects the drawing but allows for new work to be applied over the spray surface. I can set a drawing aside and then go back and add new color to the work.

Figure 9.1. This bluebird pattern shows the effect that layers of colored pencils can create. The braided vines have a brownish look even though little brown colored pencil was used. Instead, orange, yellow ochre, apple green, dark cherry red, indigo blue, and dark French gray were applied for the highlights and shadows. A thin layer of medium brown was added to the entire vine area at the end. Notice how rich the vine color looks compared to the bluebird's wing area, where only shades of blue were used.

Demonstration: Use Color to Enhance a Celtic Knot

This sample pattern is a four-line interlocking knot pattern done in tones of orange and brown colored pencil on a light ochre, textured paper background. (You can find the products listed in the supply list at most hobby and craft stores or online.) As we work through the steps to create this colored pencil work, the area contained within the white rectangle will be shown as a close-up with each step.

This is a simple half-hitch knot pattern that creates a heart shape. To create the pattern, graph out and connect the lines, as shown in the following demonstration.

SUPPLY LIST

- ❑ 80-lb. textured, acid-free, scrapbook paper (I used Rainbow Tonal CS Paper Pack.)
- ❑ Wax-based artist-quality colored pencils (I used Prismacolor Colored Pencils.)
- ❑ Acid-free white glue paste for archival work (I used Yes! Paste.)
- ❑ Reworkable spray sealer for drawings, including graphite and colored pencils (I used Reworkable Blue Label Fixatif.)
- ❑ X-acto knife
- ❑ Pencil sharpener

COLORED PENCIL CHART

- ❑ Black
- ❑ Sienna brown (medium golden brown)
- ❑ Light umber (medium brown)
- ❑ Dark umber (chocolate)
- ❑ Burnt ochre (light golden brown)
- ❑ Pale vermilion (light red orange)
- ❑ Henna (medium-dark red brown)
- ❑ White

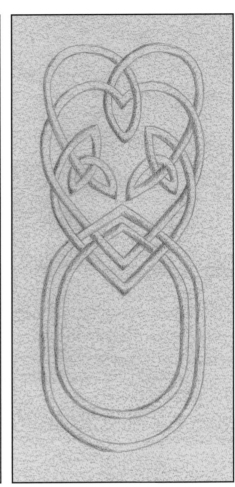

1 Make a copy of the pattern from page 135. Turn the pattern copy to the back and rub an even layer of pencil graphite over the paper. Place the pattern face up on your textured paper and lightly tape into place. With a colored ink pen, trace over the pattern lines. Do not use hard pressure during the tracing steps; the ink pen's point can cause an indent in the paper.

2 Here's the pattern transferred to the textured paper. Any additions or changes to the pattern can be made at this point using a soft No. 2 pencil.

3 Choose one side of the pattern to become the shaded side and the

opposite side of the design to become the highlighted side. For this sample, I have chosen the left side of the design to receive the shadows with the right side to be highlighted. Working a very light layer of color, use black to shade along the shadow side of the lines. About one-third of each line thickness is colored during this step.

4 On the highlighted side, shade the line with sienna brown. This shading also fills about one-third of the line area. At this point, notice that you have established the rounded-over feeling of the lines. Each line has one dark side, a pale center area, and a medium-shaded side to create that rolled-over feeling.

5 With a very sharp point, lay a thin line of black along the edge of the shaded side of the lines. With light umber, go along the outer edge of the highlighted side of the lines.

6 With dark umber, begin the shading where one line crosses under another line. Bring this shading up to touch the crossover line.

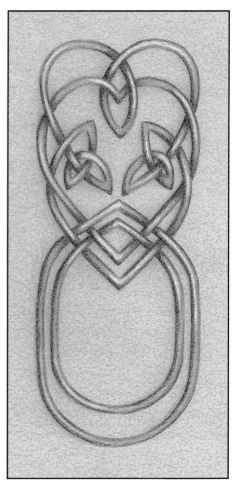

7 With white, color the center of each line at the highest point. The high point is the area of the line that crosses over another line. Use a thin, wide layering first, and then add one or two more layers just in the very center of the high area.

8 To push the lines away from the colored paper background, add a small amount of shading to the negative space surrounding the knot pattern. This step uses burnt ochre as the shading color because it is just one color tone darker than the paper color. The background or negative space coloring lies against the dark, shaded side of the line. The background space that lies against the highlighted side of the lines is not shaded.

9 A thin layer of pale vermilion has been laid over the entire line except for the center white highlights. By laying the vermilion over all of the other colors, each color becomes a tone or shade of vermilion.

10 Henna has been added to the areas of the line that tuck under crossover lines. This strengthens the shading in this area and brings the crossover shadows into a deep orange tone.

OPTIONS FOR FINISHING YOUR PROJECT

In the following examples, I've shown several different techniques that you can use once you've mastered the basics of colored pencil work. Each of these different finishing ideas will help your final Celtic design stand out from the background that you choose.

Light on Dark Marble Effect
In this sample, the drawing was done on an extremely dark-colored background paper. To bring the knot work off the paper, the shading tones begin with medium-dark to medium colors. Here, I used a medium tone called peacock blue as my shadow color against the dark turquoise background. Black has been used as the shading color for the background or negative space areas.

Coloring the Background Areas
The negative space captured within a Celtic knot design is a great place to add coloring. For this pattern, the knot work has a minimal amount of medium brown shading where one line tucks under another line. Otherwise, all the color work is done in the spaces captured by the changing knot pattern.

Working the Lines with One Color
Knots can be worked in colored pencil on one color of textured paper then cut and pasted to another color of paper. This technique uses the color of the paper. In this sample, the dark rust red is the main color of the lines. By using two different paper colors, you add emphasis to the spaces between the knot lines.

Working the Lines with Multiple Colors
Many of the patterns in this book are created using more than one line to work the knot pattern. During your colored pencil drawing sessions, you can show the multiple lines in a knot pattern by making each line a new color.

Option 1: Light on dark marble effect

Option 2: Coloring the background areas

Option 3: Working the lines with one color

Option 4: Working the lines with multiple colors

CHAPTER 10

Celtic Knot Patterns

ON THE FOLLOWING PAGES, YOU'LL FIND MORE THAN 200 READY-TO-USE CELTIC PATTERNS.

These patterns show all of the Celtic knot variations discussed in the earlier chapters, including twists and braids, knotted lines, corner patterns, self-contained knots, finials, and Viking animals. Any of these patterns can be altered to create dozens of additional patterns for your own artwork, giving you the potential to create hundreds of designs. I've also included many colored examples of the patterns to give you ideas for ways to use color in your own work.

LINE PATTERNS

SIMPLE TWO-LINE TWIST

WIDE TWO-LINE TWIST

ROLLER COASTER TWIST

FENCE WIRE TWIST

DOUBLE FENCE WIRE TWIST

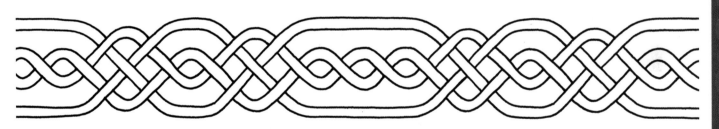

HONEYCOMB TWIST

HILL 'N' DALE BRAID

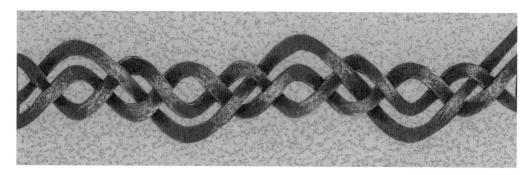

OVER THE MOUNTAIN BRAID

THREE-LINE BRAID

LINE PATTERNS

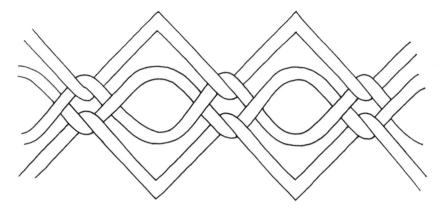

HOURGLASS TWIST

FOUR-LINE BRAID

FIVE-LINE BRAID

GARDEN PATH KNOT LINE

THICK 'N' THIN BRAID

©Lora S. Irish

SIMPLE KNOT LINE

POINTED SHOELACE KNOT LINE

SHOELACE KNOT LINE

DOUBLE POINT KNOT LINE

SEED SPIRALS KNOT LINE

SIDE-BY-SIDE HEARTS LINE

INTERLACED
HEARTS LINE

COUNTRY ROAD
HEARTS LINE

WOVEN CORDS KNOT LINE

PIXIE DANCE KNOT LINE

MERRY-GO-ROUND KNOT LINE

SUN SPIRAL KNOT LINE

ZIGZAG KNOT LINE

HARVEST MOON KNOT LINE

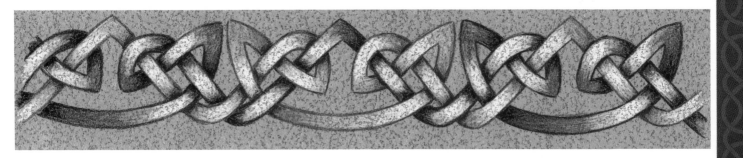

TIGHT KNOTTY PROBLEMS LINE

LINE PATTERNS

LOCKED TIGHT KNOT LINE

EYELETS AND LACE KNOT LINE

LOVER'S KNOT LINE

LOOSE KNOTTY PROBLEM LINE

TWIST 'N' TURNS KNOT LINE

PLAITED LADDER KNOT LINE

OPEN BROCADE KNOT LINE

DIAMOND LATTICE KNOT LINE

HONEYCOMB WIRE
KNOT LINE

BROCADE TANGLES
LINE

BROCADE
'N' HEARTS
KNOT LINE

©Lora S. Irish

TIC TAC TOE KNOT LINE

OVER THE RIVER TANGLE LINE

THREE BLIND MICE KNOT LINE

GREAT BOOK OF CELTIC PATTERNS

BROCADE MAZE TANGLE LINE

BROCADE MAZE TANGLE

OCEAN WAVES ORNAMENT

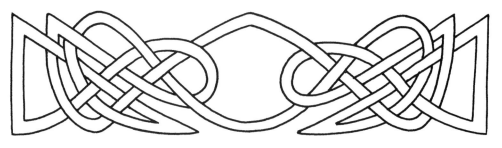

ART DECO ORNAMENT

OPEN BROCADE TANGLE LINE

OPEN BROCADE TANGLE

BROCADE LADDER LINE

CORNER PATTERNS

CORNER MOTIF 1

CORNER MOTIF 2

CORNER MOTIF 3

CORNER MOTIF 4

CORNER MOTIF 5

©Lora S. Irish

CORNER MOTIF 6

CORNER MOTIF 7

CORNER MOTIF 8

THREE-LINE BRAID CORNER

FOUR-LINE BRAID CORNER

FIVE-LINE BRAID CORNER

POINTED SHOELACE CORNER

OPEN BROCADE CORNER

WOVEN CORDS CORNER

HONEYCOMB TWIST CORNER

HOURGLASS TWIST CORNER

PLAITED LADDER CORNER

EYELETS 'N' LACE CORNER

DRAGON'S TONGUE CORNER

LOVER'S KNOT CORNER

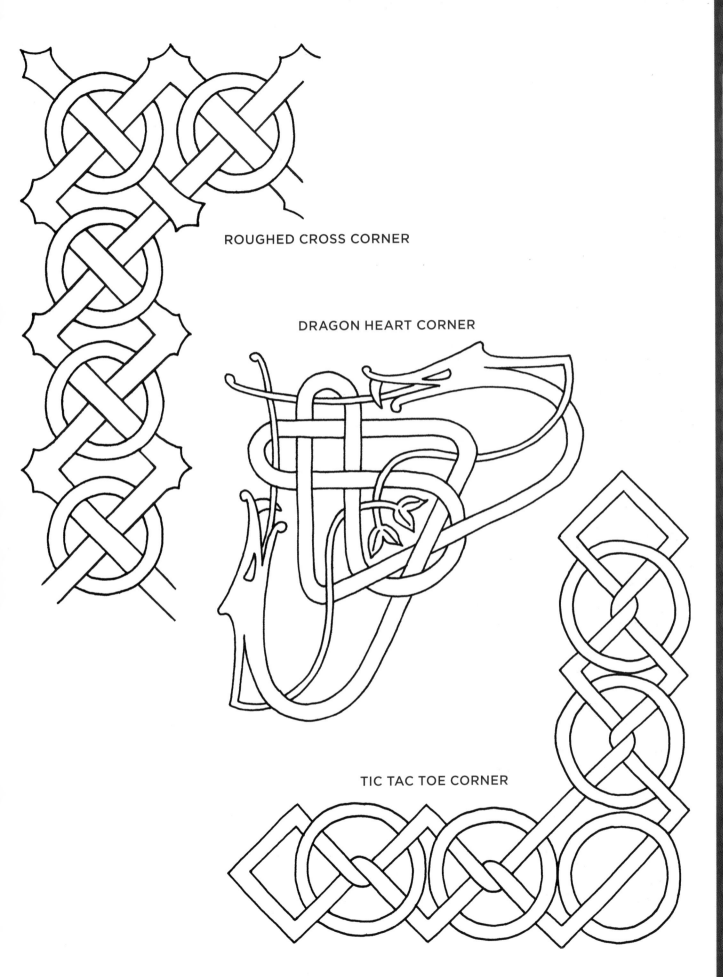

ROUGHED CROSS CORNER

DRAGON HEART CORNER

TIC TAC TOE CORNER

SUN SPIRAL CORNER

©Lora S. Irish

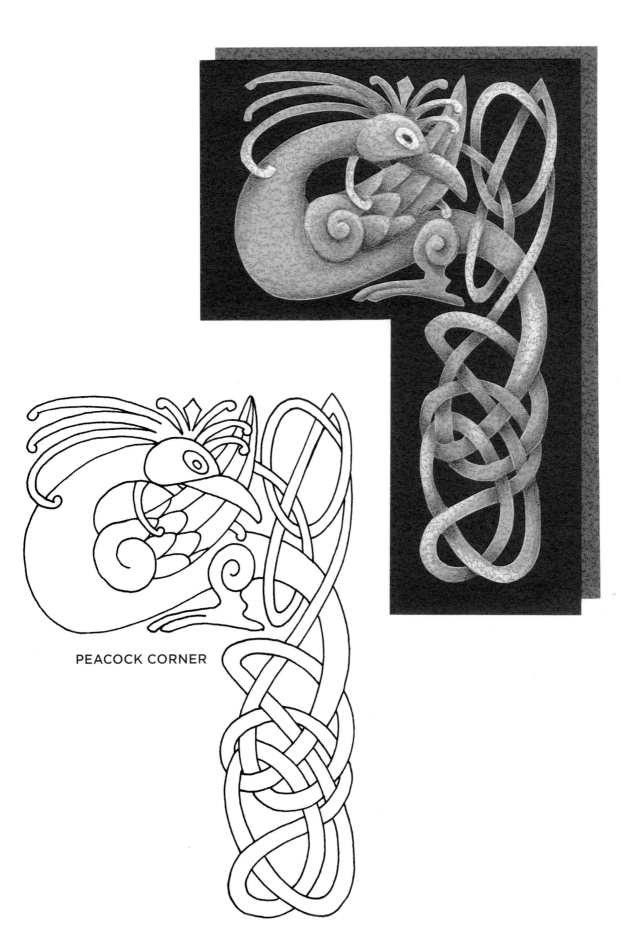

PEACOCK CORNER

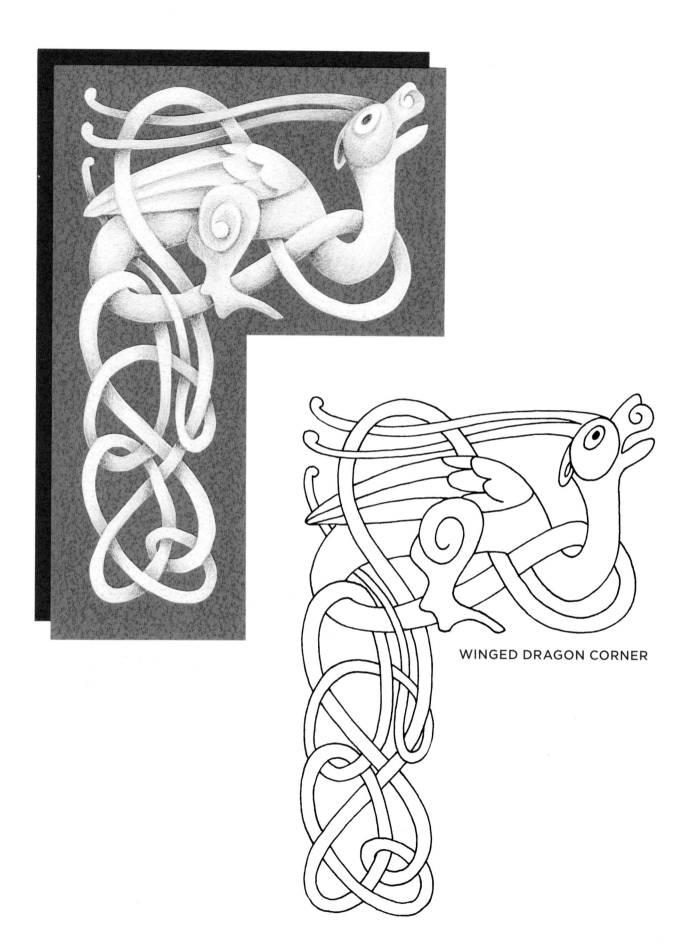

WINGED DRAGON CORNER

GREAT BOOK OF CELTIC PATTERNS

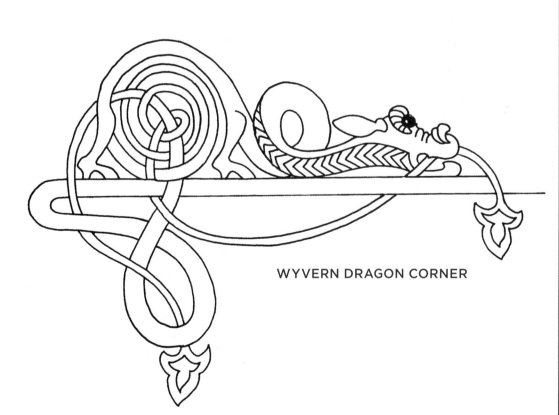

WYVERN DRAGON CORNER

DRAGON FURY CORNER

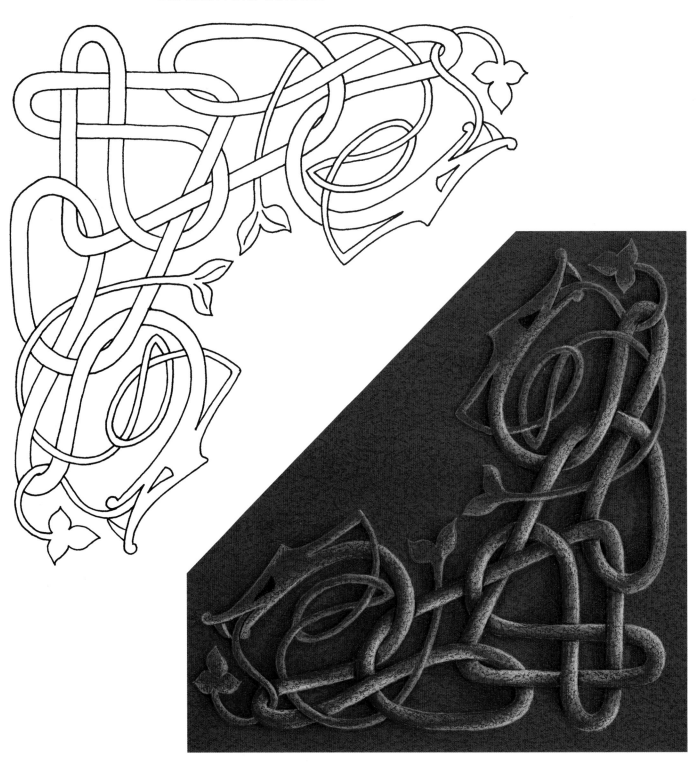

BROCADE 'N' HEARTS KNOTTED FRAME

THREE-LINE
BRAID FRAME

TAIL BITER KNOT

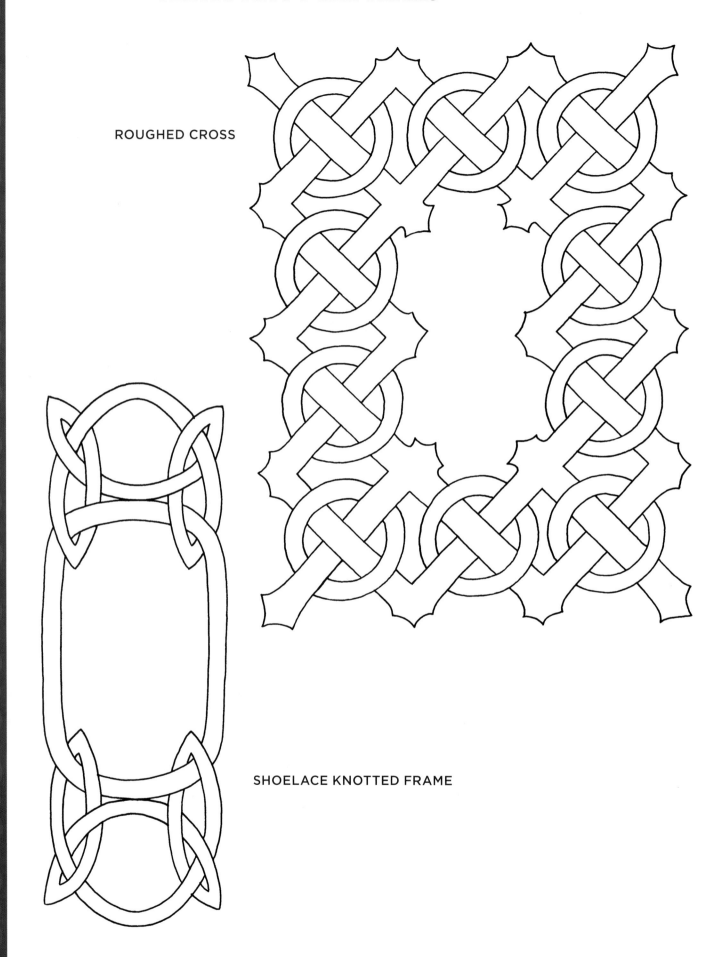

ROUGHED CROSS

SHOELACE KNOTTED FRAME

FOX AND HOUND KNOT

DRAGON FLAME KNOT

AUTUMN TWIGS KNOTTED FRAME

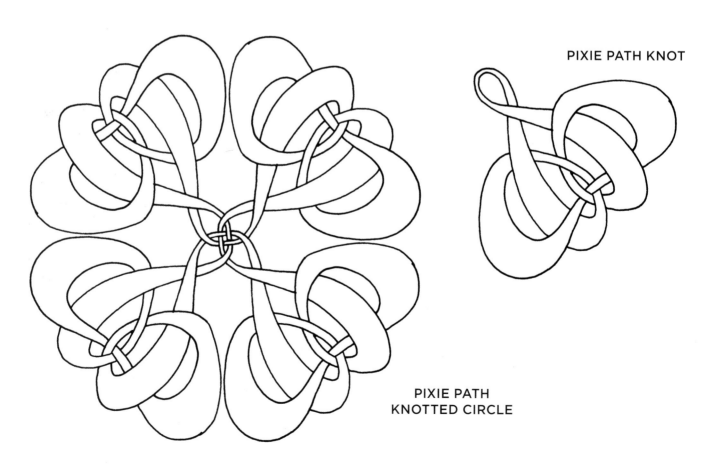

PIXIE PATH KNOT

PIXIE PATH
KNOTTED CIRCLE

©Lora S. Irish

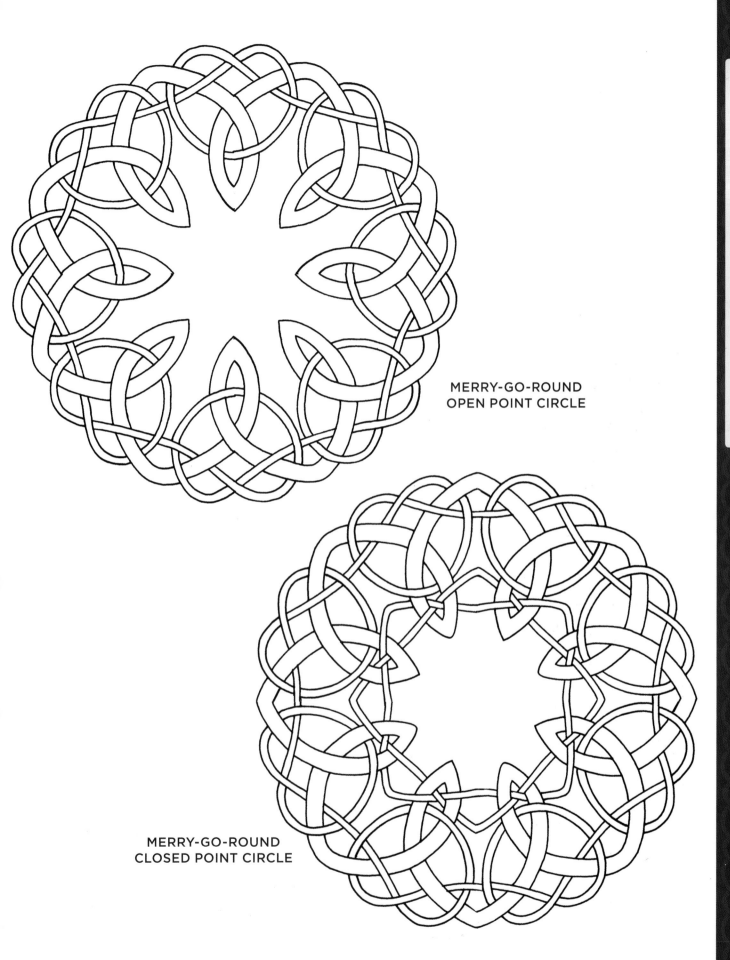

MERRY-GO-ROUND
OPEN POINT CIRCLE

MERRY-GO-ROUND
CLOSED POINT CIRCLE

HARVEST MOON DANCE FRAME

SIMPLE BOXWOOD MAZE

IRONWORK TRIVET MAZE

KING'S RANSOM KNOT

SUMMER SOLSTICE
KNOT

COMPLEX BOXWOOD MAZE

FOUR-LINE BRAID
HONEYCOMB MOTIF

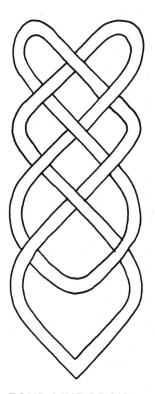

FAE'S ETERNAL PROMISE

OPEN BROCADE KNOT

SIMPLE TWO-LINE TWIST

©Lora S. Irish

COUNTRY ROAD SQUARE

INTERLACED HEARTS KNOT

THE QUEEN'S GARDEN KNOT

FICKLE MOON KNOT

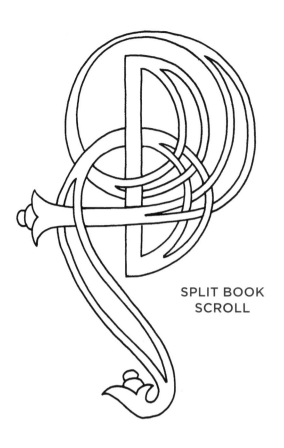

SPLIT BOOK
SCROLL

CAMEO CIRCLE ORNAMENT

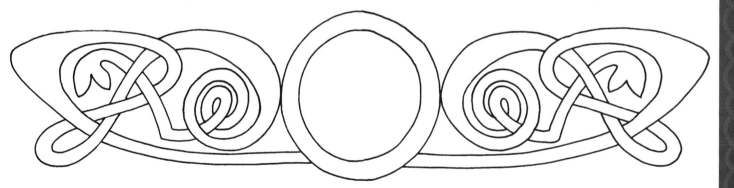

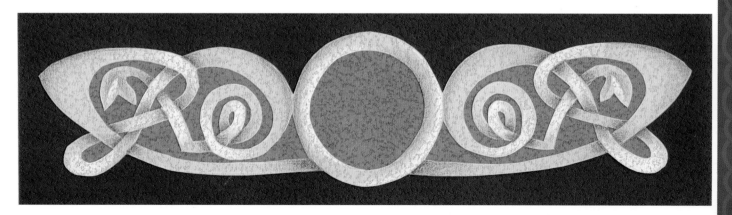

©Lora S. Irish

FOREVER LOST MAZE

ROPES AND RIGGINGS KNOT

SIMPLE CELTIC CROSS

©Lora S. Irish

BROCADE LOOPS KNOT

QUEEN'S LACE
KNOT

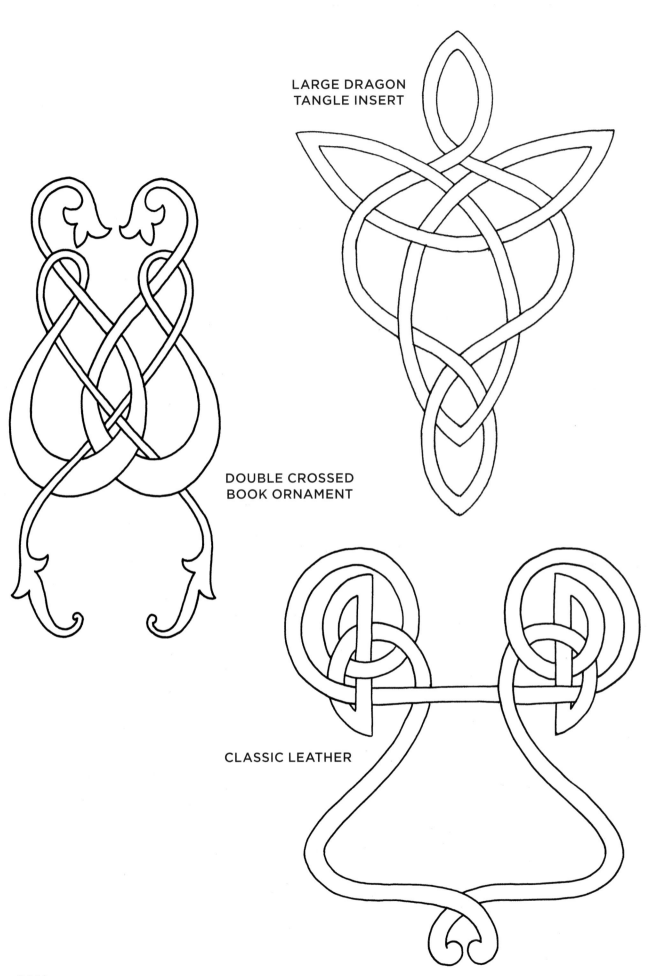

LARGE DRAGON
TANGLE INSERT

DOUBLE CROSSED
BOOK ORNAMENT

CLASSIC LEATHER

DOUBLE BIRDS

DOUBLE DRAGONS

DOUBLE HORSES

DOUBLE WOLVES

BIRD BORDER

DRAGON BORDER

GREAT BOOK OF CELTIC PATTERNS

VIKING ANIMALS

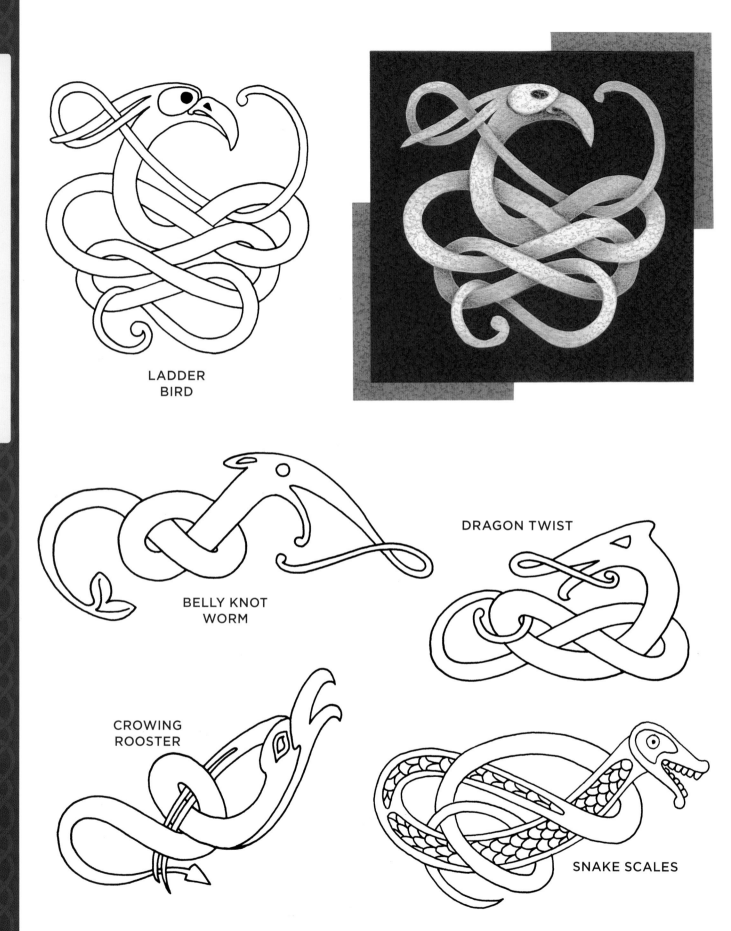

LADDER
BIRD

BELLY KNOT
WORM

DRAGON TWIST

CROWING
ROOSTER

SNAKE SCALES

VIKING SNAKE

VIKING WOLF

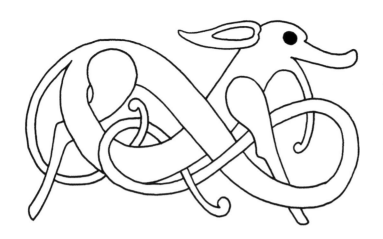

VIKING HUNTING HOUND

VIKING SNAKE PANEL

SPLIT-TAILED WOLF

JOURNAL COVER BIRD

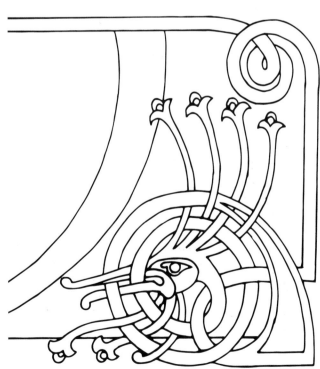

VIKING ANIMALS

LATTICE-TAILED DEER

ENTWINED WOLVES

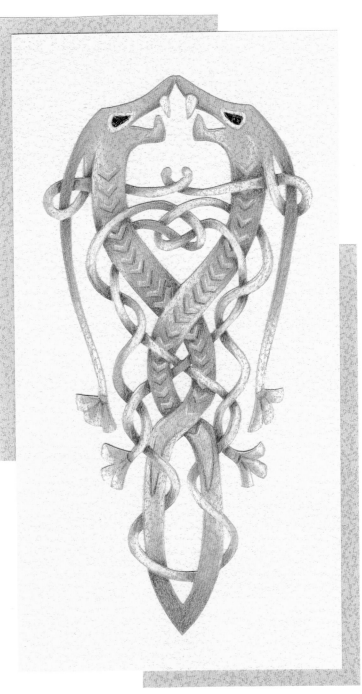

LEAF-TAILED WOLF

BROCADE DRAGON

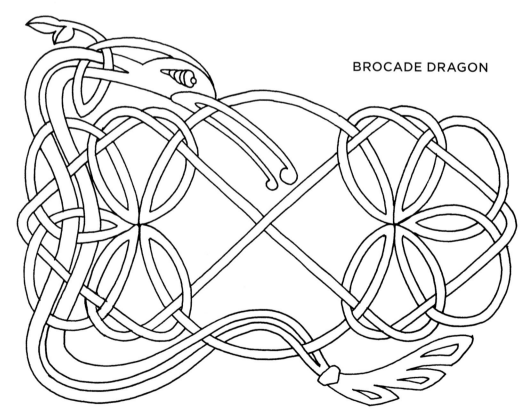

LEAF-TAILED
DRAGON

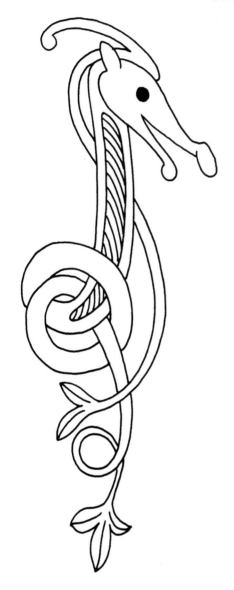

VIKING ANIMALS

PLAITED DRAGON

VIKING HART PANEL

VIKING HORSE

LARGE DRAGON TANGLE

VIKING ANIMALS

VIKING ROOSTER

TALL HART
KNOT PANEL

TANGLED BIRDS BORDER

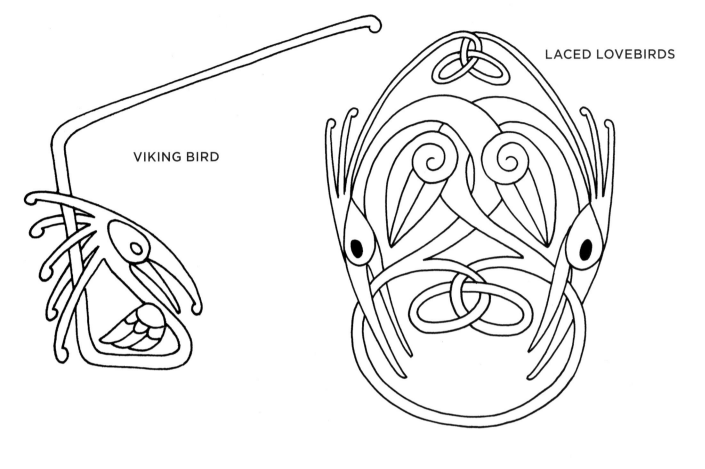

VIKING BIRD

LACED LOVEBIRDS

KNOTTED TAIL HART
PANEL

VIKING ANIMALS

LOVER BIRDS KNOT

LEAF-TONGUED LOVER BIRDS

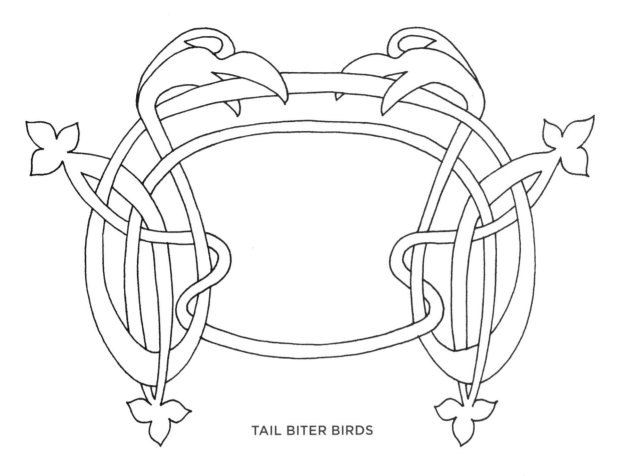

TAIL BITER BIRDS

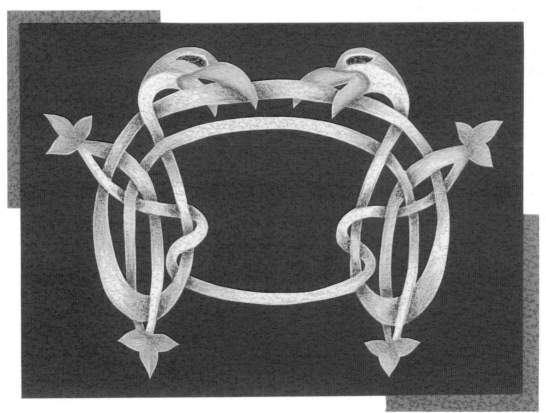

BROCADE BIRDCAGE

BIRD

GREAT BOOK OF CELTIC PATTERNS

HORSE

LION

God grant me the Serenity

STORK

GREAT BOOK OF CELTIC PATTERNS

VIKING BIRDS

VIKING WOLVES AND DOGS

VIKING ANIMALS

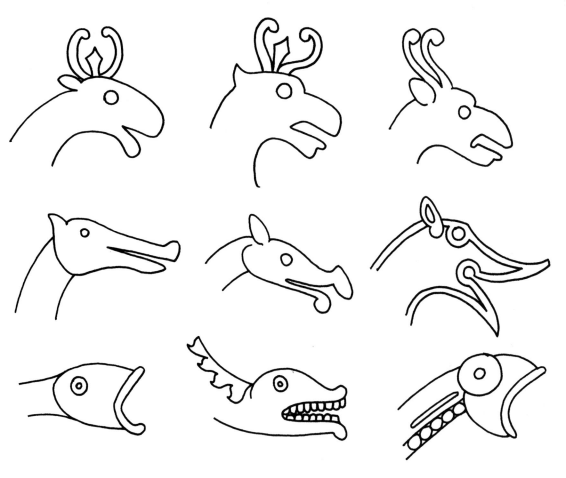

VIKING DEER, HORSES, AND SNAKES

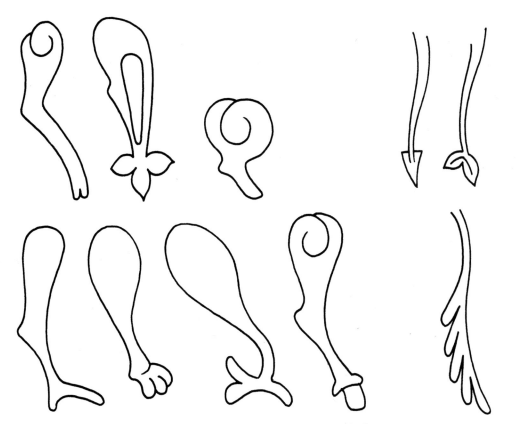

VIKING ANIMAL LEGS AND TAILS

GREAT BOOK OF CELTIC PATTERNS

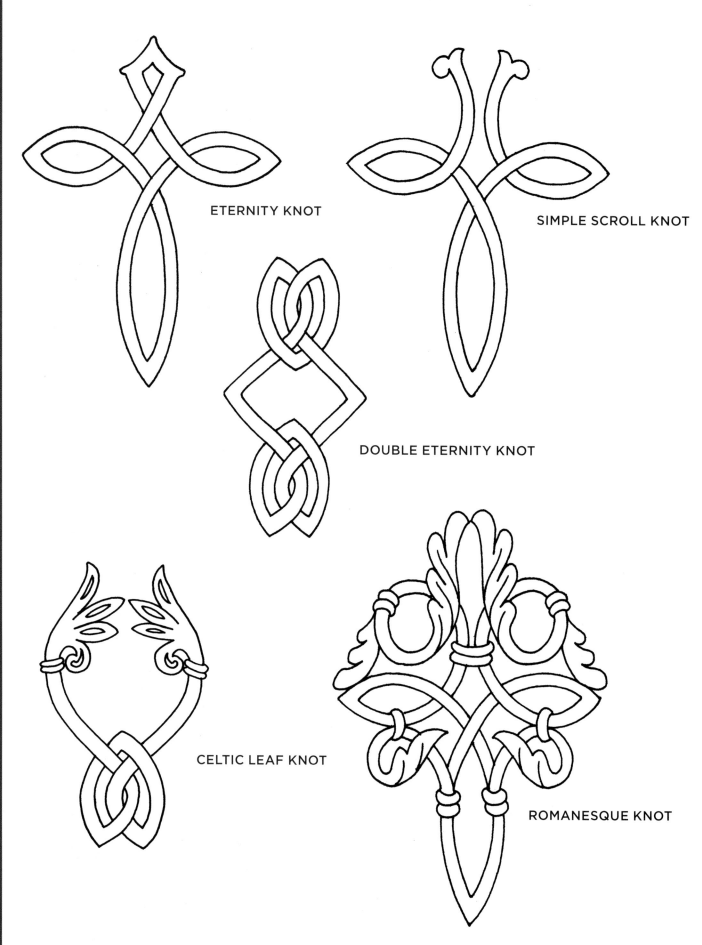

ETERNITY KNOT

SIMPLE SCROLL KNOT

DOUBLE ETERNITY KNOT

CELTIC LEAF KNOT

ROMANESQUE KNOT

GOTHIC LEAF KNOT

ITALIAN LEAF KNOT

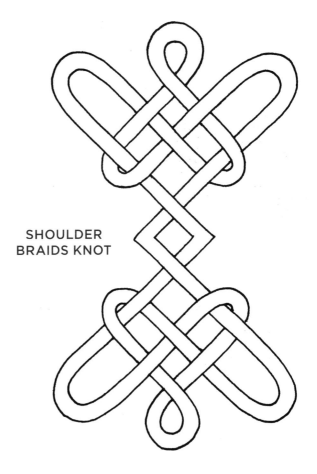

**SHOULDER
BRAIDS KNOT**

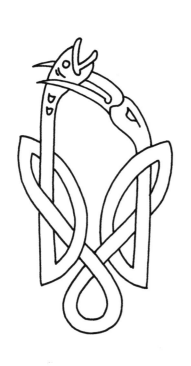

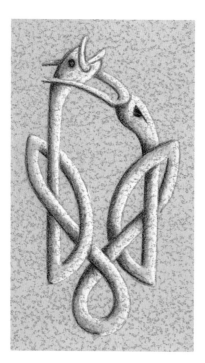

NATURE'S TALES KNOT

VICTORIAN BERRY
KNOT

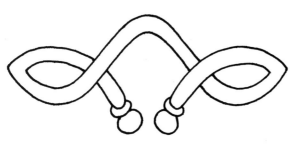

SIMPLE TWIST MOTIF

MARINER'S
KNOT

HEAVY GOTHIC LEAF KNOT

SAILOR'S
DOUBLE KNOT

CLASSIC IRISH THISTLE

PANEL KNOT

FLAGSHIP'S KNOT

GREAT BOOK OF CELTIC PATTERNS

FINIALS

LEAF AND ORGANIC FINIALS

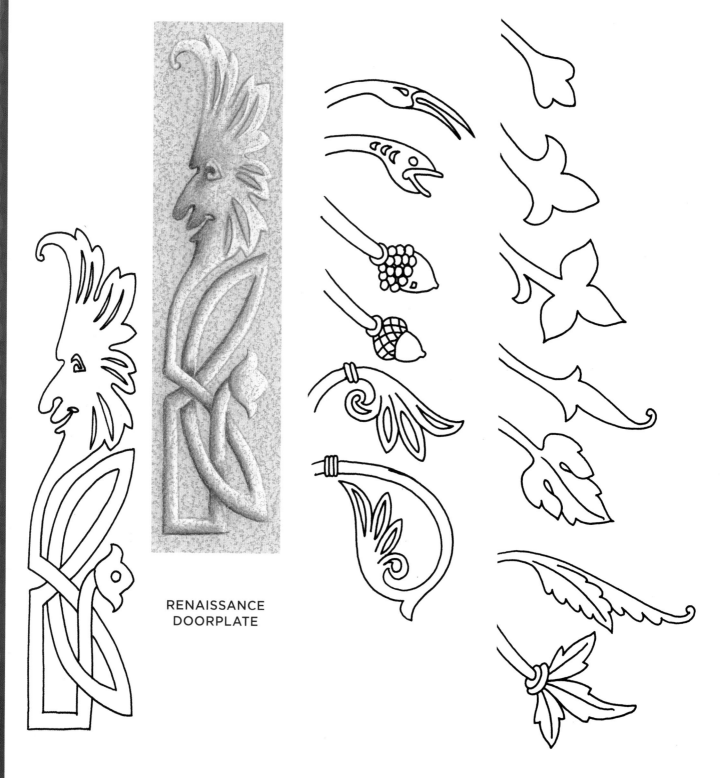

RENAISSANCE
DOORPLATE

GEOMETRIC FINIALS

BUTTERFLY
KNOT

©Lora S. Irish

LARGE THREE-LINE BRAID

BERRY BRANCHES BRAID

SAILOR'S ROPE BRAID

GRAPEVINE BRANCHES

DOUBLE-LINE BRAID

THICK 'N' THIN BRAID

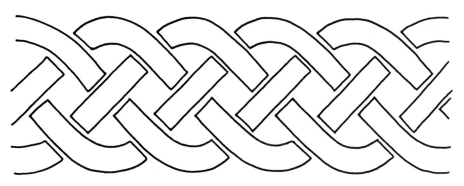

STENCIL BRAID

ORNAMENTAL LINE BRAID

MOTIF INTERSECTIONS BRAID

ACCENTED HONEYCOMB BRAID

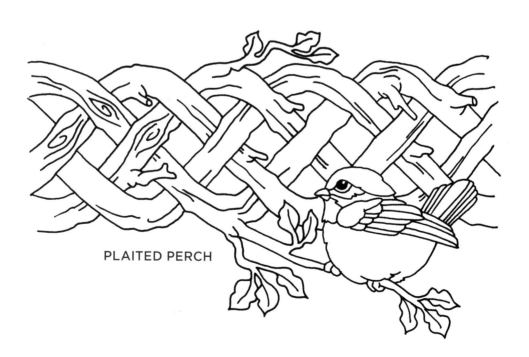

PLAITED PERCH

PLAITED PERCH ACCENT BRANCH

TREE OF LIFE

GREAT BOOK OF CELTIC PATTERNS

©Lora S. Irish

HORSE AND
DRAGON CHESSBOARD

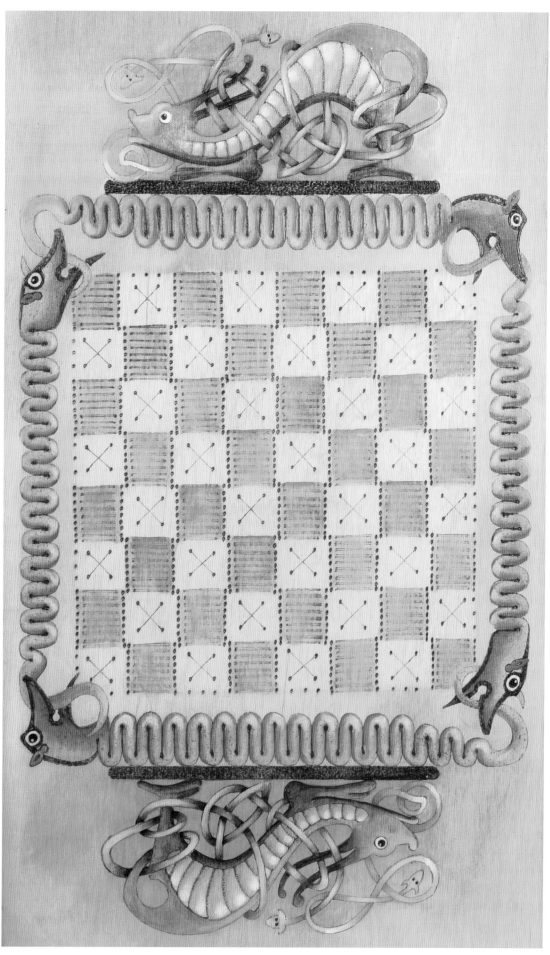

PARCHMENT PAPER DRAGON

LOVEBIRDS
PANEL

CELTIC HUNT FRAME

GREAT BOOK OF CELTIC PATTERNS

GREEN MAN, WOLVES, AND BIRDS PANEL

VIKING KING AND HORSE PANEL

FANTASY

FANTASY

SUN DOOR TOPPER

DRAGON
HEADBOARD

SUMMER SOLSTICE
DANCE

GREAT BOOK OF CELTIC PATTERNS

DRAGON
FLIGHT

PASSING THROUGH

FANTASY

TIME'S A-WASTING

CELTIC WINGED DRAGON

FANTASY

FANTASY

FOUR-LINE TWINED
HEART SPOON

TWISTED VINE FRAME

LATTICE SPATULA

LARGE HEART SPATULA

BIRD-IN-A-CAGE FORK

FANTASY

BACKGAMMON BOARD

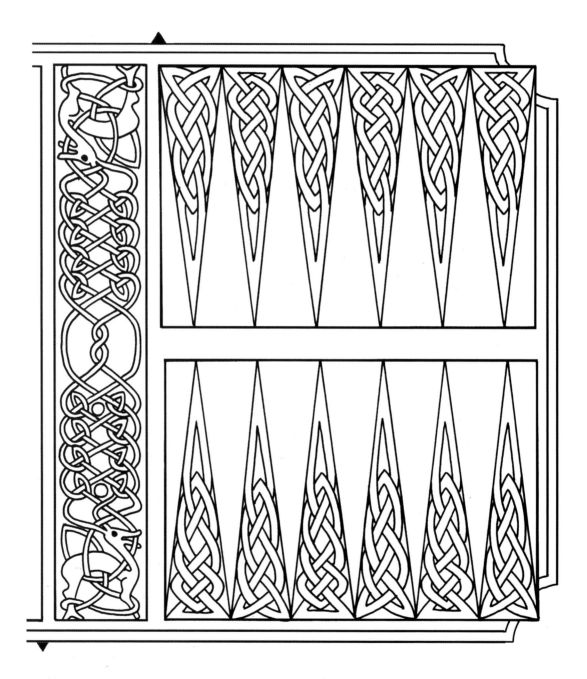

©Lora S. Irish

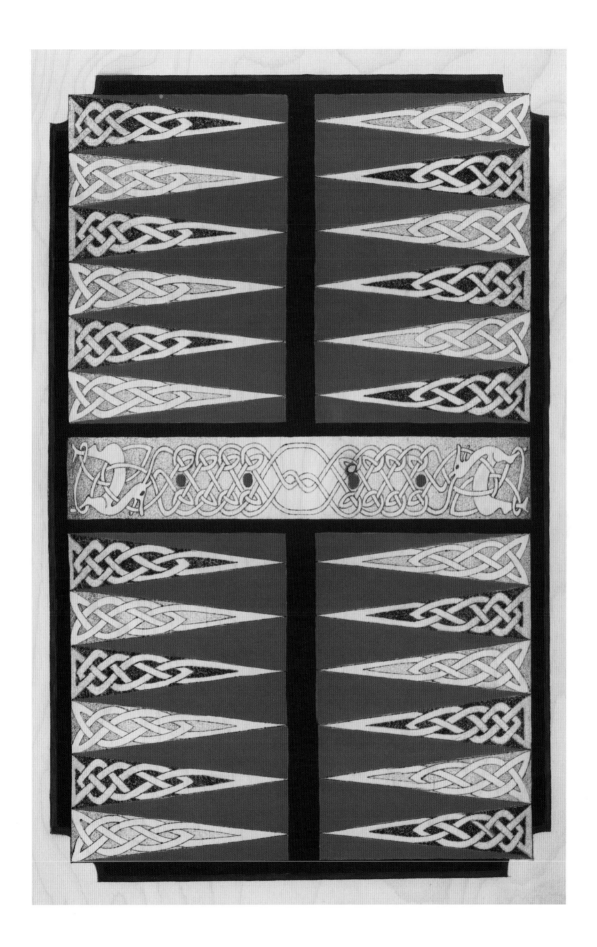

©Lora S. Irish

RELIGIOUS SYMBOLS

CELTIC CROSS 1

STONE CELTIC CROSS

©Lora S. Irish

CELTIC CROSS 2

CELTIC WINGED ANGEL

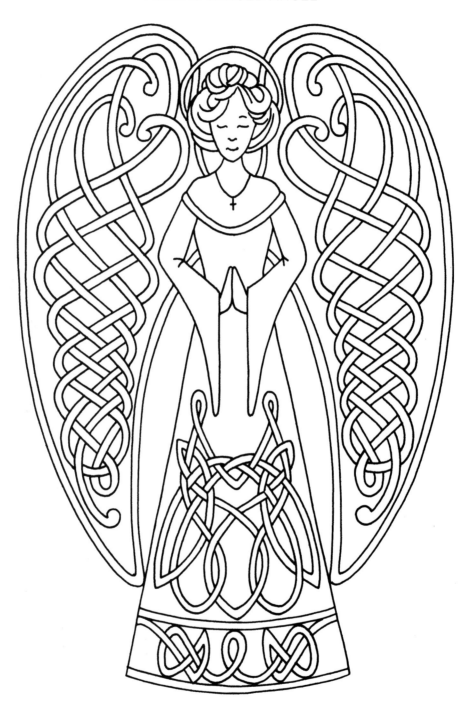

GREAT BOOK OF CELTIC PATTERNS

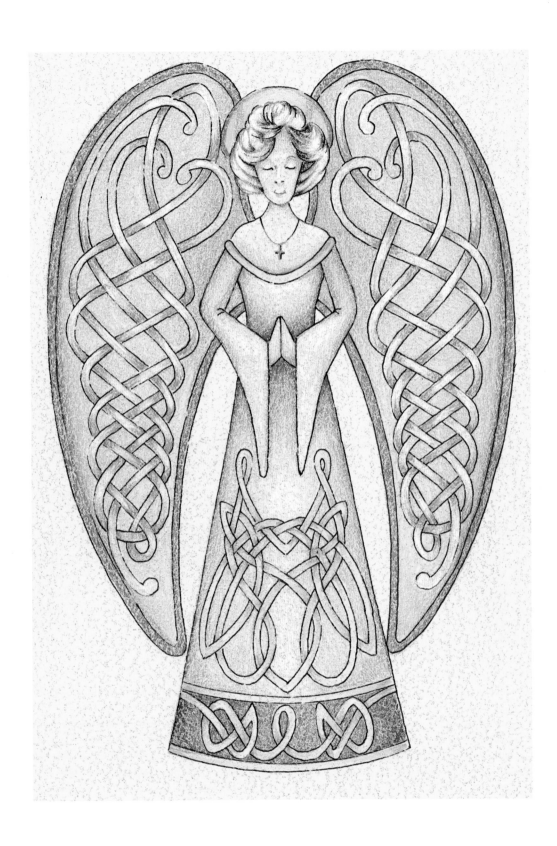

ANGEL KEYSTONE
FRAME

HERON CROSS KNOTS

Note: The patterns on this page can be used with *Heron Celtic Cross* on page 212.

HERON CELTIC CROSS

QUILT CROSS

GREAT BOOK OF CELTIC PATTERNS

©Lora S. Irish

GLOSSARY OF TERMS

Braids: Interlacing three or more lines creates a braided pattern, which is slightly more complicated than a twist. Braids are usually worked with an evenly repeated spacing, but you can vary this spacing. Braids work well in borders, straight edges, curves, and corners.

Finials: Small designs that can be added to the open or broken end lines to complete the patterns. In this pattern, the scroll leaves, shown in red, are finial designs that finish off the pattern. Finials can determine the historic art style of your finished pattern.

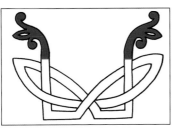

Imperfect Weave Pattern: Any Celtic line design that does not have a perfect weave pattern. These patterns will sometimes contain an area that breaks the rhythm of the lacings, which often happens when two independent line patterns are overlapped to create a frame effect or when a new design is added to the knot pattern. Imperfect weaves can be avoided by adding new lines to the design in pairs, one new line to go "over" and the second new line to go "under" the original line work. The Viking King and Horse Panel design pictured combines

three designs and uses an imperfect weave pattern. A four-line braid pattern that interlocks with a pair of Viking horses is used to create the frame, and a Viking king design is contained inside that frame. Because the tail of one horse crosses the tail of the mirror image horse to complete the frame, the over-and-under rhythm is lost at that point in the design.

Inserted Unit: A self-contained circle, square, or diamond that is interlocked within an open-ended line or another, larger, self-contained knot pattern. This four-line braid pattern has an inserted unit in the shape of a diamond, shown in blue.

Interlace or Interlacing: To weave one independent line over then under another independent line to create a twist, braid, or knot open-ended pattern. The red line is woven in an over-and-under pattern when that line intersects another line in the pattern. This over-and-under rhythm is worked throughout the entire design.

Interlock or Interlocking: To join two or more self-contained knot patterns into a new design. One self-contained knot pattern is shown in red, and it is interlocked with the knot pattern shown in blue. Lines can be made up of one repeated self-contained knot pattern or different knot patterns.

Knots: When a line turns back upon itself to create interlacing. Knots can be created using only one line or using several lines. They can be as simple as one loop or as complex as multiple loops that become tangles. A knotted line allows you to fill an area or move from one design pattern to another.

GLOSSARY OF TERMS

Open or Broken Line Patterns: Designs or patterns that have unfinished or unjoined line ends. These open ends can be completed by adding animal or finial motifs.

Perfect Weave Pattern: This pattern uses the over-and-under weave throughout the entire design. If the pattern is self-contained, one line is joined to make a continuous line design, and the over-and-under pattern is maintained at the joining point. A perfect weave can be made up of any weaving pattern as long as the weave pattern is completed throughout the entire line work.

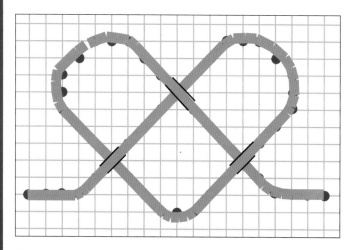

Plotting Knots: Use graph paper to create knot patterns. The scale of the graph paper acts as a guide to the size and thickness of your knotted line. Use graph paper with fewer squares per inch to get a large, thick knot. The more squares per inch, the smaller and thinner your knot will be.

Rhythm: The repeated patterns of over-and-under weaves that appear in a line that uses a repeated twist, braid, or knot design. In this repeating pattern, each intersection crosses in an identical direction to the next intersection. When creating new knot patterns, you can use the visual rhythm of the design to check if you have correctly marked your weaving pattern.

Self-Contained: Twists, braids, or knot patterns that are created using one continuous line. There are no breaks or open-ended lines.

Split Lines: Split lines can act as if they were one line going through the weaving pattern together or as independent lines that are woven separately. Parallel and split lines can be used throughout the entire design or just in certain segments of the pattern. In this pattern, each braid line is made up of two thin lines that weave over and under the other lines in the pattern as if they were one line.

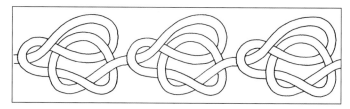

Tangles: Lines that twist, turn, and fold upon themselves without any predictable pattern and can turn back into the knot several times. Perfect for filling in large areas of work or enhancing motifs.

Twists: Simplest line designs created when two or more lines are laid one over the other to create an interlacing pattern. Twist patterns always repeat the over-and-under rhythm. The height and width of the twists can be changed, and each pattern can contain several different height and width variations.

Weaving Patterns: The number of times a line goes over then under is its weaving pattern. Most Celtic knots use a basic one-over-and-one-under pattern, but there can be variations in the weave. Just as with basket weaving techniques, Celtic knots can use a two-over-and-one-under pattern, a two-over-and-two-under pattern, or any other possible combination of weaves.

INDEX

GENERAL INDEX

Note: **Bold** page numbers
indicate patterns.

A

adding to designs

angles/points, inserted units, spiral turns, 63

color, 83–89

finials, 66–67

space and geometric designs, 80–81

textures, 78–79, 176–81

angels. *See* religious symbols

animals. *See* Viking animals

B

braids. *See also* circles, squares and motifs; corner patterns

about: overview of, 36

Accented Honeycomb, **178**

Berry Branches, **176**

Double Line, **177**

Five-Line, **95**

Four-Line, **95**

Grapevine Branches, **176**

Hill 'n' Dale, **94**

Large Three-Line, **176**

Motif Intersections, **178**

Ornamental Line, **177**

Over the Mountain, **94**

Plaited Perch, **178–79**

Sailor's Rope, **176**

Stencil, **177**

Thick 'n' Thin, **96**, **177**

Three-Line, **94**

C

changing patterns, 61–63

circles, squares and motifs, **121–37**

Autumn Twigs Knotted Frame, **124**

Bird Border, **142**

Brocade Loops Knot, **135**

Brocade 'n' Hearts Knotted Frame, **121**

Cameo Circle Ornament, **131**

Classic Leather, **137**

Complex Boxwood Maze, **127**

Corner Motifs 1-8, **108–9**

Country Road Square, **129**

Double Birds, **138**

Double Crossed Book Ornament, **137**

Double Dragons, **139**

Double Horses, 26, **140**

Double Wolves, **141**

Dragon Border, **143**

Dragon Flame Knot, **123**

Fae's Eternal Promise, **128**

Fickle Moon Knot, **130**

Forever Lost Maze, **132**

Four-Line Braid Honeycomb Motif, 15, **127**

Fox and Hound Knot, **123**

Harvest Moon Dance Frame, **126**

Interlaced Hearts Knot, **130**

Ironwork Trivet Maze, **126**

King's Ransom Knot, **127**

Large Dragon Tangle Insert, **137**

Merry-Go-Round Circles, **125**

Motif Intersections, **178**

Open Brocade Knot, **128**

Pixie Path Knotted Circle, **124**

Queen's Garden Knot, **130**

Queen's Lace Knot, **136**

Ropes and Riggings Knot, **133**

Roughed Cross, **122**

Shoelace Knotted Frame, **122**

Simple Boxwood Maze, **126**

Simple Celtic Cross, **134**

Simple Two-Line Twist, **128**

Split Book Scroll, **131**

Summer Solstice Knot, **127**

Tail Biter Knot, **121**

Three-Line Braid Frame, **121**

color, adding, 83–89

corner patterns, **108–20**

Corner Motifs 1-8, **108–9**

Dragon Fury, **120**

Dragon Heart, **115**

Dragon's Tongue, **114**

Eyelets 'n' Lace, **114**

Five-Line Braid, **110**

Four-Line Braid, **110**

Honeycomb Twist, **112**

Hourglass Twist, **113**

layout ideas, 55–59

Lover's Knot, **114**

Open Brocade, **111**

Peacock, **117**

Plaited Ladder, **114**

Pointed Shoelace, **111**

Roughed Cross, **115**

Sun Spiral, **116**

Three-Line Braid, **110**

Tic Tac Toe, **115**

Winged Dragon, **118**

Woven Cords, **111**

Wyvern Dragon, **119**

crosses. *See* religious symbols

D

dragons. *See* circles, squares and motifs; corner patterns; fantasy; gallery; Viking animals

F

fantasy

Backgammon Board, 12, **204–5**

Celtic Hunt Frame, **187**

Celtic Winged Dragon, **200**

Dragon Flight, 10, **194–95**

Dragon Headboard, **192**

Green Man, Wolves, and Birds Panel, 11, **188–89**

Horse and Dragon Chessboard, 13, **182–83**

Lovebirds Panel, **186**

Parchment Paper Dragon, **184–85**

Passing Through, **196–97**

Scales and Tails, **201**

Summer Solstice Dance, **193**

Sun Door Topper, **192**

Tail Knot Dragon, 18, **191**

Time's A-Wasting, 16, **198–99**

Twisted Vine Frame, **202**

Viking King and Horse Panel, 19, **190**

Welsh Love Spoons, 14, **203**

finials, 66–75, **170–75**

adding to designs, 66–67

geometric, **175**

larger knots as, 73

recognizable symbols as, 72

Renaissance Doorplate, **174**

various styles of, 69–75, **170–75**

Viking animals as, 68

finishing projects, options, 89

frames. *See* circles, squares and motifs; fantasy; religious symbols

G

gallery, 9–31

glossary of terms, 215–17

H

history, of Celtic knots, 1–7

about: overview of, ix

Borre stage, 4, 5, 6

early art, 2, 4

Jelling stage, 4, 5, 6

Mammen stage, 5, 6

modern art, 5, 7

Oseberg/Broa period, 4, 6

overview, 1

Ringerike stage, 5, 6

timeline, 4–5

Urnes stage, 5, 7

Viking influences, 2–7

I

inserted units, 39, 63

interlocking units, 39

K

knotted lines, 37–39

Art Deco Ornament, **106**

Brocade Ladder Line, **107**

Brocade Maze Tangle Line, **106**

Brocade 'n' Hearts Knot Line, **104**

Brocade Tangles Line, **104**

Country Road Hearts Line, **99**

Diamond Lattice Knot Line, **103**

Double Point Knot Line, **97**

Eyelets and Lace Knot Line, **102**

Garden Path Knot Line, **96**

Harvest Moon Knot Line, **101**

Honeycomb Wire Knot Line, **104**

Interlaced Hearts Line, **99**

Locked Tight Knot Line, **102**

Loose Knotty Problem Line, **103**

Lover's Knot Line, **102**

Merry-Go-Round Knot Line, **100**

Ocean Waves Ornament, **106**

Open Brocade Knot Line, **103**

Open Brocade Tangle Line, **107**

Over the River Tangle Line, **105**

Pixie Dance Knot Line, **100**

Plaited Knot Line, **103**

Pointed Shoelace Knot Line, **97**

*See*d Spirals Knot Line, **98**

Shoelace Knot Line, **97**

Side-by-Side Hearts Line, **98**

Simple Knot Line, **97**

Sun Spiral Knot Line, **100**

Three Blind Mice Knot Line, **105**

Tic Tac Toe Knot Line, **105**

Tight Knotty Problems Line, **101**

Twist 'n' Turns Knot Line, **103**

Woven Cords Knot Line, **100**

Zigzag Knot Line, **101**

L

layout ideas, 55–59

line enhancements, 77–81

line patterns. *See also* braids; knotted lines

about: overview of, 34

inserted units, 39, 63

interlocking units, 39

line twists, 34–35

Double French Wire, **93**

French Wire, **92**

Honeycomb, **93**

Hourglass, **95**

Roller Coaster, **92**

Simple Two-Line, **92**

Wide Two-Line, **92**

M

modern Celtic art, 5, 7

motifs. *See* circles, squares and motifs

P

plotting and graphing knots, 41–53

breaking pattern into multiple lines, 50–53

complicated patterns from plotted designs, 46–49

new pattern from plotted pattern, 44–45

simple knot patterns, 42–43

R

religious symbols

Angel Keystone Frame, **210**

Celtic Cross 1, **206**

Celtic Cross 2, 17, **207**

Celtic Winged Angel, **208**–9

Heron Celtic Cross, **212**–13

Heron Cross Knots, **211**

Quilt Cross, **214**

Stone Celtic Cross, **206**

S

space, adding to designs, 80–81

space, filling, 63

splitting lines, 62

squares. *See* circles, squares and motifs

stretching lines/loops, 63

symbolism, about, 7

T

tangles. *See* circles, squares and motifs; knotted lines

texturing patterns, 78–79, 176–81

twists. *See* line twists

V

Viking animals, **144**–69

birds, 22, 25, 27, 31, **144, 147, 154**–59, **160**–61, **168**

deer, **148, 169**

dragons, **143, 144, 150**–52, **153**

as finials, 68

horses, 24, 26, **140, 152, 162**–63, **169**

legs and tails, **169**

lion, 28, **164**–65

lovebirds, **155, 156**

snakes, **144**–45, **146, 169**

stork, 29, 31, **166**–67

wolves and dogs, **145**–46, **147, 149**–50, **168**

Viking influences, 2–7

A

Accented Honeycomb Braid, **178**

Angel Keystone Frame, **210**

Art Deco Ornament, **106**

Autumn Twigs Knotted Frame, **124**

B

Backgammon Board, 12, **204–5**

Belly Knot Worm, **144**

Berry Branches Braid, **176**

Bird (Viking), 25, 27, 31, **160–61**

Bird Border, **142**

Brocade Birdcage, 20, **158–59**

Brocade Dragon, **150**

Brocade Ladder Line, **107**

Brocade Loops Knot, **135**

Brocade Maze Tangle Line, **106**

Brocade 'n' Hearts Knot Line, **104**

Brocade 'n' Hearts Knotted Frame, **121**

Brocade Tangles Line, **104**

Butterfly Knot, **175**

C

Cameo Circle Ornament, **131**

Celtic Cross 1, **206**

Celtic Cross 2, 17, **207**

Celtic Hunt Frame, **187**

Celtic Leaf Knot, **170**

Celtic Winged Angel, **208–9**

Celtic Winged Dragon, **200**

Classic Irish Thistle, **173**

Classic Leather, **137**

Complex Boxwood Maze, **127**

Corner Motifs 1-8, **108–9**

Country Road Hearts Line, **99**

Country Road Square, **129**

Crowing Rooster, **144**

D

Denim Vest Viking Bird, **155**

Diamond Lattice Knot Line, **103**

Double Birds, **138**

Double Crossed Book Ornament, **137**

Double Dragons, **139**

Double Eternity Knot, **170**

Double French Wire Twist, **93**

Double Horses, 26, **140**

Double Line Braid, **177**

Double Point Knot Line, **97**

Double Wolves, **141**

Dragon Border, 23, **143**

Dragon Flame Knot, **123**

Dragon Flight, 10, **194–95**

Dragon Fury Corner, **120**

Dragon Headboard, **192**

Dragon Heart Corner, **115**

Dragon Twist, **144**

Dragon's Tongue Corner, **114**

E

English Honeycomb Braid Sugar Scoop, 15, **94**, **127**

Entwined Wolves, **149**

Eternity Knot, **170**

Eyelets and Lace Knot Line, **102**

Eyelets 'n' Lace Corner, **114**

F

Fae's Eternal Promise, **128**

Fickle Moon Knot, **130**

Five-Line Braid, **95**

Five-Line Braid Corner, **110**

Flagship's Knot, **173**

Forever Lost Maze, **132**

Four-Line Braid, **95**

Four-Line Braid Corner, **110**

Four-Line Braid Honeycomb Motif, **127**

Four-Line Twined Heart Spoon, 14, **202**

Fox and Hound Knot, **123**

French Wire Twist, **92**

G

Garden Path Knot Line, **96**

Geometric Finials, **175**

Gothic Leaf Knot, **171**

Grapevine Branches, **176**

Green Man, Wolves, and Birds Panel, 11, **188–89**

H

Harvest Moon Dance Frame, **126**

Harvest Moon Knot Line, **101**

Heavy Gothic Leaf Knot, **172**

Heron Celtic Cross, **212–13**

Heron Cross Knots, **211**

Hill 'n' Dale Braid, **94**

Honeycomb Twist, **93**

Honeycomb Twist Corner, **112**

Honeycomb Wire Knot Line, **104**

Horse (Viking), 24, **162–63**

Horse and Dragon Chessboard, 13, **182–83**

Hourglass Twist, **95**

Hourglass Twist Corner, **113**

I

Interlaced Hearts Knot, **130**

Interlaced Hearts Line, **99**

Ironwork Trivet Maze, **126**

Italian Leaf Knot, **171**

J

Journal Cover Bird, 22, **147**

K

King's Ransom Knot, **127**

Knotted Tail Hart Panel, 21, **155**

L

Laced Lovebirds, 16, **155**, **198–99**

Ladder Bird, **144**

Large Dragon Tale, **153**

Large Dragon Tangle Insert, **137**

Large Three-Line Braid, **176**

Lattice Spatula, 14, **203**

Lattice-Tailed Deer, **148**

Leaf and Organic Finials, **174**

Leaf-Tailed Dragon, 15, **151**

Leaf-Tailed Wolf, **150**

Leaf-Tongued Lover Birds, **156**

Lion (Viking), 28, **164–65**

Locked Tight Knot Line, **102**

Loose Knotty Problem Line, **103**

Lovebirds Panel, **186**

Lover Birds Knot, **156**

Lover's Knot Corner, **114**

Lover's Knot Line, **102**

M

Mariner's Knot, **172**

Merry-Go-Round Closed Point Circle, **125**

Merry-Go-Round Knot Line, **100**

Merry-Go-Round Open Point Circle, **125**

Motif Intersections Braid, **178**

N

Nature's Tales Knot, **172**

O

Ocean Waves Ornament, **106**

Open Brocade Corner, **111**

Open Brocade Knot, **128**

Open Brocade Knot Line, **103**

Open Brocade Tangle Line, **107**

Ornamental Line Braid, **177**

Over the Mountain Braid, **94**

Over the River Tangle Line, **105**

P

Panel Knot, **173**

Parchment Paper Dragon, **184**–85

Passing Through, **196**–97

Peacock Corner, **117**

Pixie Dance Knot Line, **100**

Pixie Path Knotted Circle, **124**

Plaited Dragon, **152**

Plaited Ladder Corner, **114**

Plaited Ladder Knot Line, **103**

Plaited Perch (and Accent Branch), **178**–79

Pointed Shoelace Corner, **111**

Pointed Shoelace Knot Line, **97**

Q

Queen's Garden Knot, **130**

Queen's Lace Knot, **136**

Quilt Cross, **214**

R

Renaissance Doorplate, **174**

Roller Coaster Twist, **92**

Romanesque Knot, **170**

Ropes and Riggings Knot, **133**

Roughed Cross, **122**

Roughed Cross Corner, **115**

S

Sailor's Double Knot, **172**

Sailor's Rope Braid, **176**

Scales and Tails, **201**

Seed Spirals Knot Line, **98**

Shoelace Knot Line, **97**

Shoelace Knotted Frame, **122**

Shoulder Braids Knot, **171**

Side-by-Side Hearts Line, **98**

Simple Boxwood Maze, **126**

Simple Celtic Cross, **134**

Simple Knot Line, **97**

Simple Scroll Knot, **170**

Simple Twist Knot, **172**

Simple Two-Line Twist, **92, 128**

Snake Scales, **144**

Split Book Scroll, **131**

Split-Tailed Wolf, **147**

Stencil Braid, **177**

Stone Celtic Cross, **206**

Stork (Viking), 29, 31, **166**–67

Summer Solstice Dance, **193**

Summer Solstice Knot, **127**

Sun Door Topper, **192**

Sun Spiral Corner, **116**

Sun Spiral Knot Line, **100**

T

Tail Biter Birds, **157**

Tail Biter Knot, **121**

Tail Knot Dragon, 18, **191**

Tall Hart Knot Panel, **154**

Tangled Birds Border, **154**

Thick 'n' Thin Braid, **96, 177**

Three Blind Mice Knot Line, **105**

Three-Line Braid, **94**

Three-Line Braid Corner, **110**

Three-Line Braid Frame, **121**

Tic Tac Toe Corner, **115**

Tic Tac Toe Knot Line, **105**

Tight Knotty Problems Line, **101**

Time's A-Wasting, **16, 198**–99

Tree of Life, 31, **180**–81

Twist 'n' Turns Knot Line, **103**

Twisted Vine Frame, **202**

V

Victorian Berry Knot, **172**

Viking Animal Legs and Tails, **169**

Viking Birds, **168**

Viking Deer, Horses, and Snakes, **169**

Viking Hart Panel, **152**

Viking Horse, **152**

Viking Hunting Hound, **146**

Viking King and Horse Panel, 19, **190**

Viking Rooster, **154**

Viking Snake, **145**

Viking Snake Panel, **146**

Viking Wolf, **145**

Viking Wolves and Dogs, **168**

W

Welsh Love Spoons, **203**

Wide Two-Line Twist, **92**

Winged Dragon Corner, **118**

Woven Cords Corner, **111**

Woven Cords Knot Line, **100**

Wyvern Dragon Corner, **119**

Z

Zigzag Knot Line, **101**

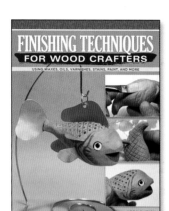
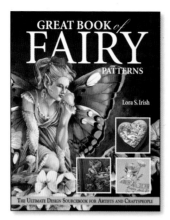

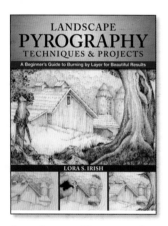
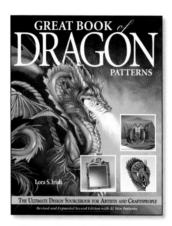